STRAIGHT TALK
FROM
THE BIG WINNERS

In today's fast-moving, rough-and-tumble, high-pressure world of professional sports, it takes more than brute strength to become a superstar. It takes determination, a keen playing edge, carefully controlled aggression . . . and that one extra dimension in a player's character that makes the difference between a merely competent player and a true sports great.

The superheroes in this book—Fran Tarkenton, Bobby Richardson, Carl Erskine, Bart Starr, Juan Marichal, Felipe Alou, and many others—all have that extra dimension, and in their own words they talk straight about how it's affected their careers, their personal lives, their intimate relationships.

———————

RUNNING WITH GOD gives the reader an insider's picture of these superstars—sportsmen, Christians, human beings—and a true understanding of that extra spiritual dimension that gives them the winning edge.

Running with God

THE NEW CHRISTIAN ATHLETES

JAMES C. HEFLEY

SPIRE BOOKS

RUNNING WITH GOD: *The New Christian Athletes* is an original publication of Avon Books. This work has never before appeared in book form.

AVON BOOKS
A division of
The Hearst Corporation
959 Eighth Avenue
New York, New York 10019

ISBN: 0-380-00541-7

First Avon Printing, November, 1975
Third Printing

AVON TRADEMARK REG. U.S. PAT. OFF. AND
FOREIGN COUNTRIES, REGISTERED TRADEMARK—
MARCA REGISTRADA, HECHO EN CHICAGO, U.S.A.

Printed in the U.S.A.

Contents

CHAPTER ONE

The New League

SUPER BOWL WEEK—MIAMI

Booze, sex, and bets for many of the fans, hustlers, and promoters in Sun City, U.S.A., for America's closest competitor to the Roman circus.

But not for the performers at Dade Junior College Stadium.

Here the hoopla begins with a prayer and an Olympic-style march of one hundred clean-living college athletes marching four abreast around the track. Next come fifty cross-country bikers, followed by the superstars—over one hundred pro athletes who prefer the New Testament to *Playboy*.

The pros—some who will be playing in the upcoming Super Bowl V—turn and stride down the center of the gridiron to be introduced to a cheering, screaming crowd of teen-agers.

Two big-name stars speak. Jerry Stovall, who was then a Cardinal defensive back, is applauded when he acknowledges the Man from Nazareth as the "Coach of my life. When I'm in doubt about what to do in a situation, I always ask myself, 'Would Jesus do it?'" Then Jim Kaat, the freckled, 25-game winning pitcher in the American League, is honored by a quiet reverence as he recalls the "emptiness and void" that follows great victories. "Knowing Jesus Christ has helped fill that vacuum for me," he declares.

But none of the gridiron and diamond favorites can compete with spine-tingling demonstrations staged by two specialty stars.

Mike Crain, a judo and karate black belt holder, shivers the teens with his sword thrusts. First he slashes a watermelon in half on the stomach of Bob Anderson, running back for the Denver Broncos, while Anderson keeps smiling. "I never lost confidence in Mike," he says. "I knew he had the help of the Lord."

Then Crain whips the sword through the bright sunlight again and slices a banana on the outstretched hand of Ohio State's All-American running back Leo Hayden. "I was saying the Twenty-third Psalm," Hayden confesses to the awed crowd.

Forth comes gargantuan Paul Anderson, a legendary modern "Atlas" touted as the "strongest man in the world." An Olympic gold medalist in weight lifting, Anderson also holds the record for the most weight ever lifted on the back of any man—6270 pounds.

"America is split," the bearish man with a 24-inch neck, 36-inch thighs, and 60-inch chest shouts, and illustrates this opinion by pounding a nail through a two-by-four with his bare fist. "The only way to overcome this problem is to turn to God. The way to turn to God is through Jesus Christ. He can make us love one another."

Eight high-school huskies leap on a table. Anderson brings gasps from the youthful audience by lifting them, table and all, in the air. Putting the groaning table down gently, he makes another point: "The strongest man does not stand upon the Olympic pedestal. The strongest Man alive is Jesus Christ because He can change the human heart. He is the only One who has the answer for life. He is my strength." Then dropping his voice, he challenges, "Never be ashamed that you are a Christian."

Calvin Jones, the smallest player at cornerback in the National Football League, steps forward. At five feet, seven inches and 169 pounds, he can be easily lifted by Paul Anderson in one hand. "We aren't pushing any religious group," the Denver Bronco star tells the kids. "But we are saying that God wants each of you to have an abundant life. You can have that life through Jesus Christ."

After Jones comes Atlanta Falcon linebacker Don Hansen to give a talk on drugs. "Why settle for an artificial high," he argues, "when Jesus Christ can give you the real thing?"

Twelve more pro football players give advice that young people usually turn off when coming from parents and community authorities. There are no whistles or catcalls. No scuffling in the aisles or walking out. Just respectful silence that breaks only when they split to watch a football scrimmage between the visiting pros and a team of local university seniors.

EASTER VACATION, DAYTONA BEACH, WHERE THOUSANDS OF COLLEGIANS FLOCK FOR SUN, SURF, BEER, AND FOR SOME—SEX

A jazz band rips out with "The Saints Go Marching In." When a crowd gathers, Paul Anderson does his lifting trick and says, "It takes a man to follow Christ."

The band plays another hot number, then Baltimore Colt linebacker Don Shinnick (now a defensive coach for the Oakland Raiders) steps onstage and invites questions.

Q. "How can you say God is love when He sends hurricanes and tornadoes to kill people?"

A. "God doesn't kill anyone. He allows these things to happen within the natural order of events. I can't fully explain why because I'm not a philosopher or a theologian. But I do know that in God's eternal way of thinking there is no catastrophe in the Christian life. And I do believe the Bible when it says. 'All things work together for good to them that love God.'[1]

"Let's bring it down to a personal level. We've lost some big football games by what seemed to be twists of fate. I don't know why. Make it even more personal with me. A few years ago my wife Marsha gave birth to twins. We named them Peter and Joel. Peter after the apostle. Joel, for the Old Testament prophet. A couple of days later little Peter picked up a staph infection in the hospital and died. Marsha and I were crushed, but we found comfort in prayer and believing that on God's level of thinking it was best."

Q. "Do you always pray to win a game?"
A. [*Smiling*] "I sure don't pray to lose. I ask the Lord to help me do my best and glorify Him."
Q. "What's wrong with sex?"
A. "None of us have said anything is wrong with sex, have we? I think it depends upon the time and the purpose and who you have it with. For me, it's wrong outside of marriage."

That evening, Shinnick, Anderson, old pro Bill Wade (he quarterbacked the Chicago Bears to their last National Football League championship in 1963), and magician Joe Hale go to a nightclub where they had made arrangements earlier to speak. When the emcee introduces them, everything stops. Even the go-go girls sit and listen as the visitors talk about a different life from what most of the audience lives.

The next day there is more jazz, speaking on the beach, and person-to-person dialogue. One young man sports a jaunty sweater lettered STAMP OUT VIRGINITY. Team member Loren Young, a staff member of the Fellowship of Christian Athletes (FCA) stops the boy and says, "Hey, that's a neat sweater. Don't ever throw it away. Keep it and take good care of it until you have a grown-up daughter. Then give it to the first fellow who takes her out."

The boy pales, but walks on by without mumbling a word. Later in the day—without the sweater—he seeks out the FCA staffer. "I'll never wear it again," he pledges. "Thanks for teaching me something."

PROFESSIONAL FOOTBALL GAME IN BALTIMORE

Colt cornerback Rex Kern, one of Ohio State's all-time signal callers, tackles a ball carrier running along the sidelines near his bench. The action happens so fast it's hard to tell if Kern has brought the runner down within bounds. While Kern is getting up, an assistant coach runs over and vents his fury in angry, locker-room language. Kern, who has made "a one-hundred-percent commitment to live for Jesus Christ," isn't amused. "Coach, that's terrible language for you to be using," he admonishes.

The coach pulls back and waits for the other coaches and players to give support. No one does.

WORLD SERIES, 1971: SECOND GAME IN BALTIMORE BETWEEN THE ORIOLES AND THE PITTSBURGH PIRATES, WITH THE ORIOLES HAVING LOST THE FIRST GAME, 5-3.

Baltimore has already scored five runs in the fifth inning. With Dave Johnson on second base, the batter singles to left. Left-fielder Willie Stargell fields the hard-hit ball. Johnson rounds third and scoots for home.

Pirate catcher Manny Sanguillen takes Stargell's bullet throw and blocks the plate with his left leg, ready to tag the oncoming runner.

Realizing that to slide means a certain out, Johnson never breaks stride and slams into the little Panamanian catcher. If he hits Sanguillen hard enough, the catcher will drop the ball.

For an instant Sanguillen wants to cream the runner.

Back in Panama when he was a boxer and street fighter, he would have sent such a runner up for jaw surgery. Now the new Sanguillen takes control and the fans see him crawl from under Johnson with a smile on his face and the ball in his mitt.

"In the old days, it would have been bang!" the little catcher tells a sportswriter afterward. "Now I don't want to take revenge."

So it goes with the new breed of athletes on God's squad.

They don't fit the stereotype many fans hold of athletes, especially pro players.

As a few pro athletes are reputed to do, they don't play tag in their shorts with half-naked girls in hotel corridors. Or get snockered on the first break from team discipline. Or get thrown into hotel swimming pools at three a.m. Or hang around bars, or associate with known gamblers. Or kick, bite, or scratch underneath the pile after the whistle has blown. Or curse in the shower and putrefy their opponents' ancestry. Or scowl and walk away from little boys who have been waiting outside the dressing-room door for an hour, hoping for a pen scratch from their heroes. Or spend every waking moment scheming to make more money. Or endorse products in which they honestly do not believe, or beat their wives, seduce the spouses of other men, and neglect their children.

And they don't like to emphasize negatives of Christianity, but the positives—peace, joy, fulfillment, and the satisfaction of feeling they are bettering the human race.

Actually Christian athletes feel the image of the most notable swingers is greatly overdrawn. Don Maynard, who has caught more Namath passes than any other receiver, thinks Broadway Joe's night life has been "blown out of proportion to sell tickets." Maynard suggests that fans "multiply" what they've heard or read about Namath's ability and "divide" everything else. Still, he concedes that he and the Jets long-haired quar-

12

terback do have different life-styles. Maynard is as square in his convictions as the cornerstone of a Texas courthouse, a family man who prays with his children, and a teetotaler who vows he has never even gulped a beer.

Roger Staubach blames a permissive society for the overpurpling of athletes. "The type of movies and magazines that are popular indicate that people are looking for something unusual in the sexual way," he says. "That carries over into athletics."

Staubach doesn't appreciate some of the epithets applied to him by magazines. "I'm not sure I like the implications that I'm a fanatic or an ascetic. I enjoy some of the same things Namath does. You know sex is a part of my life, except it's channeled in a different department.

"For myself, I believe we are here for something more than just for today. This philosophy is my whole life. If being a square means being a Christian and living by Christian principles and values, if it means being considerate of people and being faithful to your wife, well, then, I'm a square."[2]

Staubach's capsule comments are echoed by hundreds of other athletes in all sports—college, amateur, and professional.

"I want to be a Christian athlete," drawls Dodger pitcher Don Sutton whose 209 strikeouts his first big-league year were the highest of any rookie since 1911. The jug-eared Mississippi country boy, who was termed by departing Sandy Koufax "the key to the team's success," isn't one to shove his beliefs down a teammate's throat. "I know a man can be a good athlete without being a Christian," he says, "but I think he can be a better one as a Christian."[3]

Bart Starr agrees. The former University of Alabama and Green Bay Packer quarterback and recently appointed coach of the Packers thinks that an athlete who is spiritually fit and concerned about others will be a better performer in the contest. "That's because you're at peace with yourself," Starr says, adding that an ath-

13

lete who is not in shape spiritually will be out of balance and possibly suffer emotional upheavals and other problems.

John Havlicek put it more succinctly when responding to an award as the outstanding sports figure in Ohio after the Boston Celtics won another world professional basketball title: "All the composure and poise people say that I have comes through the presence of Jesus Christ in my life."[4]

Pat Williams, the new general manager of the Philadelphia 76ers, contrasts his philosophy with a secular definition of winning in life. "How do you know you're winning?" the modish basketball promoter asks. "By the number of cars or television sets you have? By the size of your net worth? By the number of people you have influence over or can regulate? By the trophies in your den? Some of the richest people I know are the most miserable. I've heard that the average income of the thousands of people who commit suicide each year is twenty-five thousand dollars. No, money and power and fame don't make you a winner or bring real meaning to life. For me, you're only winning when you know Jesus Christ personally and are committed to His way of life."

These and many other highly visible Christian sports figures are not spouting pious clichés. They represent a growing force in a world of organized sports threatened by commercialism and greed. Though a minority, their influence is felt far beyond their numbers. They are leaders on college and pro teams. For example, Roger Staubach, one of the most respected, is quarterback of the Dallas Cowboys. Many coach for major universities. Tom Landry, who knows his Bible almost as well as he does his playbook, is trail boss of the Dallas Cowboys. Many more are assistant coaches.

The Fellowship of Christian Athletes has been the major catalyst in welding Christianity and sports together for a winning combination. Consider that FCA will involve 10,000 young athletes in 28 summer camps this year. They will come to play and pray and listen to their heroes, who give their services free. During the school term, the FCA network will stretch to include 1500 high-school Huddle groups, 250 college Fellowships, and another 250 supportive adult Chapters.

Consider also that most major professional football and baseball teams now hold Sunday-morning chapel services on the road. Anywhere from five to fifty team personnel assemble—usually in a rented hotel room—for a devotional talk, prayer, and discussion of a Bible passage.

In baseball alone twenty-two of the twenty-four major-league clubs now hold player chapels before Sunday games. Much of the impetus has come from former *Detroit News* sports writer Watson "Waddy" Spoelstra, founder of Baseball Chapel, Inc. Spoelstra joined the Christian athletes' team back in 1957 after his critically ill daughter was "miraculously healed." Before that he had been a hard-drinking writer who covered hotel bars as well as he did games for his paper.

Spoelstra recruits team members to be chapel leaders and to help select speakers for their pregame worship services. Pitcher Don Sutton, for example, leads the Los Angeles Dodgers. Power hitter Reggie Jackson, who got turned on by black evangelist Tom Skinner, is the surprising chapel spark plug for the Oakland Athletics. The A's and the Dodgers both held worship services as usual before the Sunday game of the 1974 World Series. Reverend William Pannell, a professor from Fuller Theological Seminary in Los Angeles, spoke to both clubs separately.

Sometimes the fans are involved. For example, the Oakland A's sportcaster Monte Moore got A's owner Charles O. Finley's permission to hold a fifty-minute pregame service on Easter Sunday. "It's important to let others know of our beliefs," he says.[5] Bobby Richardson, second-baseman hero from the days of New York Yankee glory, delivered a ringing sermon to ten thousand Bay area fans.

Many more are hearing the Christian athletes speak out in big-city rallies, sports interviews, talk shows, and

Christian team tours, under the auspices of FCA, Campus Crusade for Christ, and other groups. Americans are becoming aware that these athletes stand for values that will endure long after the cheers of the stadium crowds have died away.

Who are they? What makes them different from other jocks who continue to excite the fans in this sports frenetic age? What do they believe? How do they feel about sex, drinking, race relations, violence on the playing field, a win-at-all-costs philosophy, and other issues? Why do they feel the Christian way is best for them among the myriad of competing ideologies?

We will attempt to answer these and other questions about the Christian athletes in chapters to follow.

CHAPTER TWO

The Great Commitment

Manny Sanguillen rivals Johnny Bench as the best catcher in baseball. The lightning-fast little hustler from Panama won more All-Star votes than Bench in 1972 and was the National League's first-team catcher that year. And in the heat of the 1974 pennant chase, teammate Dock Ellis said, "We need him because we can't win without him." Manny doesn't brag about himself or claim to be a self-made man. He does point to a life-changing experience at nineteen "when I met Jesus Christ."

Nobody back in Colón, Panama, would have picked Manny as most likely to succeed. His family was dirt poor. His father drank too much. Manny started work at thirteen, often slaving from dawn to dusk for thirty-five cents an hour. When not working or sleeping, he roamed the streets picking fights, drinking, romancing, gambling.

Then he saw a slim, gray-haired foreigner preaching on a street corner. "You can have a new life. You can be a new person," Reverend Elmer Fehr, a Canadian missionary, was saying. "Turn to Jesus Christ who died on a cross for your sins. Believe in Him. Stand up for Him. He will make you new."

Intrigued, Manny and some other boys hung around to meet the preacher personally.

"Come over to my house tomorrow," the Canadian invited, giving them his address. Besides Manny and his brother, three other boys went.

"I want to organize a baseball team," the preacher said. "Will you boys help me?"

"Sure," Manny volunteered even though he had played only basketball and soccer.

The team they put together was a winner. Soon they were going into Panama City to play. By this time the missionary and his wife had practically adopted Manny.

On spare evenings they spent long hours discussing the Bible. But it wasn't just what Manny learned that turned his life around. It was the love and peace he felt in their home. One evening he prayed and committed himself to "follow" Jesus Christ.

He was thinking of going to a seminary in Mexico City when a Pittsburgh Pirate scout saw him play in Panama City. Impressed, the scout offered a contract. Manny talked it over with his spiritual mentor who suggested that he might be more beneficial to the cause of Jesus Christ by playing ball than preaching from a pulpit. Manny went to Florida for spring training in 1965. Six years later he was playing in the World Series.

"My life belongs to God," Manny says. "One hundred percent. We go up and down in baseball, but God never changes."

It is this personal faith—commitment to God through Christ—that the Christian athletes, Protestants and Catholics, share. Christianity to them is not a brief token of time given up to God on Sunday morning. It is a day-by-day deepening of relationships, vertically with God and horizontally with fellow believers.

Besides Manny Sanguillen, a surprising number of other Spanish-speaking baseball players have made this commitment. The most influential among them is the veteran Felipe Alou, the eldest of three big-league brothers, who also helped former teammates Juan Marichal and José Pagan understand the Christian way.

Alou had little interest in Christianity when growing up in the Dominican Republic. When he left to play baseball, a boyhood friend who had recently become a Christian gave him a Bible. Alou thanked him and buried the book in his belongings.

While playing minor-league ball in Florida and Louisiana, he chafed over racial discrimination. The racial taunts and provocations in towns dotted with Christian churches troubled him so much that he almost gave up baseball. But he persevered and found better times when the Giants called him up to play in the big leagues.

It rained the day he was scheduled to play his first game with the Giants, and he sat in his hotel room reading telegrams from fans in the Dominican Republic. One was from Rocque Martinez, the friend who had given him the Bible. Besides congratulating Felipe, Rocque reminded him that he would "find that baseball is not everything . . . even a big-league ball player needs Christ."

Alou was moved by his old friend's concern. He was sure the telegram had cost half a week's wages. There in his hotel room he prayed for God to show him how to become a Christian. Then he dug out the gift Bible and began reading.

Later pitcher Al Worthington spotted Felipe poring over the gift Bible in a hotel lobby. Having recently been converted in a Billy Graham meeting, he approached the new player and pointedly asked, "Are you a Christian?"

Felipe looked up and smilingly shook his head. "But I'm trying to understand how," he said.

Extending a brawny hand, Worthington suggested they study the Bible together. On the next road trip, Worthington and Alou concentrated on the New Testament. Finally Felipe said he believed in Christ but couldn't be sure that the Man from Nazareth would accept him.

They returned to San Francisco for a series of home contests. The Dominican continued his search. One day in his room at the Whitcomb Hotel, he was thinking about Romans 10:13. *It says "whosoever" calls upon*

*Christ will be saved. I have called upon Him. "Whoso-
ever" is me. Will He accept me? Yes, He promised. Can
I trust His promise? If I can't, who can I trust?*

Suddenly his eyes gleamed with understanding. It
was trust, faith—not a certain feeling! He was a Christian.

Felipe couldn't wait to share the simple but profound
discovery with his Southern friend. He went immediately to the park where Worthington was warming up
and ran across the infield to the pitcher's mound.

Worthington knew it by the glow on his friend's face.
"You've found it! You're sure!" he announced before
Felipe could babble a word.

"Yes, yes, I'm saved! I'm a Christian now. If God
said it, that's enough!"

The spectators must have wondered what new baseball strategy the two were discussing as they stood arm
in arm.

Felipe immediately began sharing his new faith with
his brothers and other Latin players. José Pagan, his
on-the-road roommate, was one of the first to accept the
new life. He and Felipe kept Bibles by their bedside,
surprising more than one sportswriter who came to their
room for interviews.

Felipe returned home to Santo Domingo as a national
sports hero. On a television sports program he was
asked, "What was your greatest moment in baseball?"
Surprisingly, he did not speak of a game-winning home
run or a spectacular catch. "It was when I accepted
God's promise and became a Christian," he said and
went on to describe the new peace and self-assurance
that had resulted.

There are miles of cultural distance between Felipe
Alou and the urbane, methodical Tom Landry. The
Dallas Cowboys' coach has been dubbed a plastic man
and "Mr. Computer Face" because of his lack of emo-
tion when the fans are in pandemonium. Actually,
gentleman Landry is just thinking ahead three or four
plays. Under different circumstances he can laugh, or
cry, or even tell a Texas yarn. But almost always he has

his emotions under superb control. His wife Alice has never even seen him get mad at their kids.

When you ask him the secret, he'll point you to the same person who changed Felipe Alou's life: Jesus Christ. "Since 1958 He's been the center of my life. If I'm fulfilling His plan in every activity, I don't have to worry very much about what happens."

Landry was already a good coach before making the great commitment. His skill in reading enemy formations gave the New York Giants the NFL championship in 1956 when he was their defensive coach. The Giants almost repeated the victory in 1958, before losing in sudden-death overtime to the stubborn Baltimore Colts.

Even before the loss of the championship, Landry had been feeling vaguely dissatisfied. He had reached every goal he had ever sought, but still something seemed missing.

One day he was asked by a friend, Frank Phillips, if he'd like to attend a men's Bible study breakfast at the Melrose Hotel in Dallas. An off-and-on church member, Landry wasn't sure he wanted to go. But he turned up at 7:30 on a Wednesday morning in the hotel dining room and halfheartedly entered into the discussion of a Bible passage. After a few minutes he found himself enjoying the jovial exchanging of views. Bible study became interesting.

He returned to the Bible study every Wednesday. Soon enjoyment turned into personal concern as he reflected on a verse from the Sermon on the Mount: "Therefore I tell you, do not be anxious about your life, what you shall eat or what you shall drink, nor about your body, what you shall put on. Is not life more than food, and the body more than clothing?"[1]

The application to his life was plain. Jesus was saying there was something more important in life than winning football championships, making a pile of money, attaining status.

More important than being a head coach—his next goal in life? He reflected further. Yes, that must be included, too.

The conclusion shook him hard, but he kept going back.

One morning they examined Jesus' parable of the wise and foolish builders.[2] The wise man's house on the rock had not been moved by the floods, while the foolish man's house on the sand had been swept away. The foundation had made the difference.

The parable left him unsettled and unsure that he had been building on the right foundation. But who was Jesus to say he hadn't been pursuing the right course? Was He all that He claimed to be? Did He deserve unwavering respect and obedience?

Tom Landry was not a man to dismiss a hard question lightly. For the first time in his life he carefully studied the results of Jesus' teaching, death, and supposed resurrection. He compared the Nazarene to other personages of history. In his opinion no philosopher, writer, potentate, or religious leader had influenced history as Jesus had.

Now he faced the hardest decision of all. Should he fully commit his life to Jesus as Lord and Savior or continue putting lesser goals first?

There was no dramatic, cliff-hanging crisis, no time or sacred place which he can now stake out in his recollection. "I just found myself more and more drawn to Jesus until I let Him take over every area of my life, including football. Over a period of time I discovered true joy and satisfaction."

Then just as Landry was losing his all-consuming desire to become a head coach, he was contacted by Tex Schramm, the newly hired general manager of the new Dallas Cowboys franchise. Over lunch, Schramm offered Landry the head coaching job.

Now after sixteen years of highs and lows in his profession, Landry is more certain than ever that he made the right commitment in building his life around Christ. The sum purpose of life, he still believes, is "finding the right relationship with Jesus Christ. When He became real to me and I looked at life His way, I found real happiness and the most satisfying purpose for living."[3]

Basketball's Bill Bradley is a lot like Tom Landry—steady, reliable, disciplined, and gifted with a razor-sharp mind. Because of his commitment to Christ, he also has spiritual priorities in his life.

Bradley's early religious experiences were in a small-town Missouri Presbyterian church his banker father and mother attended. His mother taught Sunday school and led the choir.

The first stirrings in Bill's religious cocoon came after his junior year in high school when he attended a Fellowship of Christian Athletes' camp in Lake Geneva, Wisconsin. "I went to meet all my sports greats and to improve myself in athletics," he recalls, "But I found the camp was fifty percent inspiration."

Testimonials of faith by James Jeffries (who put on an eye popping juggling act), pro quarterback Fran Tarkenton, and other sports heroes moved Bradley to look beneath the veneer of Christianity. Jesus Christ became more than a name voiced in hymns and creeds.

Bradley returned excited. He could hardly wait for his friends to hear the tapes of the conference speeches he had brought home. But the rush of senior activities soon wore his spiritual impressions thin, and he lapsed back into the old religious routine.

He went back the next summer and got charged up again by inspirational speeches from his heroes. He made a stronger, though still shallow, commitment.

A six-foot, five-inch high-school All-American who had scored 3066 points in his prep career, the poised, dark-haired banker's son was a college coach's dream. He received seventy-five scholarship offers. At the last minute, he chose Princeton over Duke, even though the Ivy League school had not been among the seventy-five.

Self-confident and assured, he arrived at Princeton brimming with ambition. Then troubles began dogging his fast steps. He had problems with French. A broken foot did not heal as fast as he had thought it would. The future looked cloudy.

One day after a disappointing French exam, he holed up in his dorm room and tried to think out solutions to his worries. While brooding, he suddenly remembered a record made by Bob Pettit, the old basketball pro who had spoken at the last FCA camp. He flipped the disc on his portable player and listened.

"We're not playing for the state or national championship," he heard Pettit say. "We're only playing for the victory of Christ in the hearts of men."

I'm worried only about myself, the discouraged young athlete thought. *My grades, my ability to play basketball. I should be concerned about other people.*

He reflected on the life of Christ. *Everything He did was for someone else. He even gave His life as a sacrifice for others. I should really give myself to Him and start thinking of others.*

It was this awareness of his own selfishness as contrasted to the unselfishness of Christ which turned Bill Bradley in a new direction. The rangy forward moved on to become a two-time All-American and the most exciting basketball player in Princeton's history. In 1964 he was named College Basketball Player of the Year and the following year was voted Most Valuable Player in the NCAA Basketball Tournament. Playing in the 1965 tournament, he scored fifty-eight points against Wichita to set an NCAA tournament single-game scoring record.

Upon graduation from Princeton, he spurned pro offers to study in England under a Rhodes Scholarship. After completing his work abroad, he returned for a stunning career with the New York Knicks.

Bill Curry, center of the NFL's Houston Oilers, came up much like basketball's Bradley, until he got "on track" for Jesus Christ at Georgia Tech. In ten pro years Curry has played for four teams in the NFL. Not that he isn't a good center. He's one of the best at his position. Nor is he uncooperative with coaches; they can't fault his dedication to the game. It's the owners who don't appreciate his extracurricular activities. They probably would like to see him ensconced in a cozy little engineering job, far out of range of television cameras that focus on him when he says grown men don't like to be told when to go to bed.

Curry might be no more than an obscure engineer and a forgotten third-string Georgia Tech player if he had not discovered the Four Spiritual Laws in college. But we must first go back a bit.

He was nurtured in a Presbyterian home. His parents were both Sunday-school teachers. He was president of his Sunday-school class and captain of his high-school sports teams in College Park, an Atlanta suburb. "I thought I was a Christian," he confesses, "but my main idol in life was football. It was the best way I knew to glorify myself."

After graduation he drove across town and signed to play under coach Bobby Dodd at Georgia Tech. Brash and flushed with confidence, he expected to become a mainstay on the first team. Instead, he turned out to be more of a "rambling wreck" in Coach Dodd's opinion. "You don't have what it takes to be a college player," Dodd told him bluntly. "You probably won't go higher than third string."

The coach's assessment knocked Curry off his pedestal of self-worship. With his wonder-boy ego deflated, he moped around campus trying to think of ways to improve.

Summer came and the future looked no brighter. Having nothing better to do, he joined a group going to an FCA Conference in Lake Geneva, Wisconsin. The speakers listed on the program had made it. Maybe he could pick up some tips from them.

At camp the young Georgian saw himself in a different light. He realized his Christianity had been only a put-on, a lie. He had followed only a form and had never put his life on the line for Jesus Christ. Now he wanted to do that more than anything else. He prayed to receive Christ into his life, but returned home still confused.

Back in school he had an assuring conversation with Jon Braun, the Atlanta representative of Campus Crusade for Christ.

"As an engineering student, you know that physical laws govern the universe," Braun told him. "Well, there are spiritual laws that govern our relationship with God."

"Yes, that sounds sensible," Curry observed. "What are they?"

"Number one: God loves you and has a wonderful plan for your life."

"Yes, I guess He does if He loves me."

"Number two: Man is sinful."

"Number three: Jesus Christ is God's only provision for man's sin."

"I know that," Curry interrupted, "but I'm still confused."

"Number four: God invites you to accept Christ as your Savior."

"I accepted Him at the FCA camp. At least I thought I did."

"I don't doubt your word, Bill," the Crusade man said. "Maybe your problem is you've been trying to live the Christian life in your own strength."

Curry suddenly remembered something "Deacon" Dan Towler, the ex-Los Angeles Ram All-Pro back turned minister had said at Lake Geneva: "To succeed in the Christian life, you've got to let Christ live through you."

From that time Bill Curry's attitude has been, "Lord, let your life shine through me. Let me love and do for others as You would do."

The experience transformed Curry's outlook. Freed from the chains of self-interest, he became a team motivator.

The new attitude carried over into football. Coach Dodd was delighted, but also curious about how he had improved so much.

The new Bill Curry grinned shyly. "It's not a great secret, Coach. I stopped playing for myself and started playing for the Lord. I asked Him to help me work harder and get to practice earlier, and He did."

The ex-third stringer graduated as permanent captain

of his squad, won All-American honors, and was drafted by the Packers.

The Packers sold Curry to the Baltimore Colts where he met a natural friend, Rex Kern. The Ohioan, who had won a starting cornerback position his rookie year with the Colts, has also met Jesus Christ in a personal way.

The freckled barber's son from Lancaster, Ohio, dropped out of Sunday school when he was a junior-high student. He was brought back by a Sunday school teacher who genuinely loved boys and sports.

George Hickman was a factory worker. But he attended all the high-school games and on Sundays he used sports illustrations to get across the lesson.

It took little persuasion from Hickman to get young Kern into church and later to hear Billy Graham in Columbus. At the evangelist's invitation, Rex joined hundreds of inquirers going forward to declare their intent to accept and follow Christ. A crusade counselor gave him some printed Bible verses to learn and some workbooks to fill out, and encouraged him to become active in his church.

But it was George Hickman who gave him the personal guidance needed to set his feet on a straight course.

Hickman never saw his protégé become nationally famous. He died of a heart attack on his way to a high-school game. A cheerleader told Rex as he was walking to the playing field. Shaken, he vowed to become worthy of his Sunday school teacher's devotion.

Another highly visible Christian athlete is Dean Prentice, the 21-year veteran left winger for the Minnesota North Stars. Prentice was at the apex of his career when he made the great decision.

He and his wife June had prayed and attended church for years and considered themselves good, moral parents. Until an old friend of Dean's dropped by, they were certain of their purpose in life. Jim Connally and Dean had played junior hockey together in Canada.

"What are you doing?" was the natural question for Dean to ask his old buddy.

"I'm studying in Milwaukee to be a missionary," Jim replied. "Going to serve God full time. What are your plans?"

Dean had almost twenty years in the National Hockey League and was seventh-leading scorer in the league. He knew he couldn't hang on much longer. He could make money in the business world where his name would count for something, or perhaps, coach the game he knew best. But his eyes didn't shine as he talked about the future with his friend who was pursuing a higher calling.

After Connally left, Dean and June discussed their goals. "There has to be more to living than just acquiring more material things," Dean felt.

June agreed, then together they decided to take another look at the New Testament. This, in Dean's words, led them to "taking Jesus Christ into our lives."

Their commitment led to Dean's joining the Bible Study Fellowship of Minneapolis, a group of serious-minded men who discuss the Scriptures every Monday night at Mt. Olivet Lutheran Church in Minneapolis. Dean himself spends hours each week studying the Bible and preparing his lessons for the group discussions. He has also become active with FCA in Minneapolis, joining with another good friend, Fred Cox, place-kicker for the Minnesota Vikings.

He still hopes to coach, but his purpose goes beyond building a winning team. As he told the *Minneapolis Tribune*'s Dwayne Netland, "I hope to bring other hockey players to know Jesus Christ as their personal Savior."[4]

Skate champion Janet Lynn is everybody's sweetheart in the sports world. The graceful queen of world rinks has had a second home on ice since her parents took her along to Cub Scout skating parties on Chicago ponds when she was only two and a half. Now a professional, she still flashes the disarming smile of innocence. It is hard to imagine Janet Lynn otherwise.

She, too, witnesses that the center of her life is now Jesus Christ. Though her family "always" went to church, she was not always a Christian.

"I never knew what being a Christian was until I attended the Gloria Dei Lutheran Church Confirmation Camp," she confided to Gary Warner, editor of *The Christian Athlete*. "I had always wanted to do the right things, and my spiritual searching started when I was little.

"One Sunday, years ago, the sermon really touched me, and I began to cry. My dad didn't know why I was crying, and I wasn't sure either. Another night after that I was saying the Lord's Prayer before I went to sleep— as I did every evening—and I realized that I was just mouthing the words. They didn't mean anything. This troubled me.

"At Confirmation Camp we were given the Four Spiritual Laws [the same laws which helped Bill Curry]. My best friend Margie Sloan, a golfer, and I sat up until four A.M. talking about what all this meant. The next night in the service we both gave our lives to Jesus Christ.

"This was merely the tender roots of my faith. It was not an emotional reaction. I really didn't understand what I had done; I just knew I believed in Jesus ... [Now] I'm only beginning to comprehend the fullness of the Christian life. Jesus has given me meaning and peace."[5]

Such are the pivotal spiritual experiences of Manny Sanguillen, Felipe Alou, Tom Landry, Bill Bradley, Bill Curry, Dean Prentice, and Janet Lynn. Here is the terminology which they use to describe their commitment. Janet Lynn "gave" her life to Jesus Christ. Dean Prentice "took" Jesus Christ into his life. Bill Curry "prayed to receive Christ" into his life. Tom Landry found himself "more and more drawn to Jesus until I let Him take over every area of my life." "New birth" and "new creation" are the Biblical terms.[6]

The semantics are not as important as the new ongoing relationship these athletes established with Jesus

Christ. Since entering into this relationship, their intellectual and social horizons have broadened as they have grown and matured. Some who made commitments as teenagers have had time to reassess and reevaluate what happened. But their faith in Christ continues and their lifestyle continues to be ordered by moral and spiritual priorities.

CHAPTER THREE

Sex and the Christian Athletes

A half century ago the respectable media profiled all star athletes as paragons of virtue. In those days of loose understatements Frankenstein's monster might have come off as an Eagle Scout and Jack the Ripper as a delightful practical joker if they had been baseball players. The owner moguls were still reeling from the Black Sox Scandal that involved eight Chicago White Sox players with bribery in the 1919 World Series. They pressured newspapers not to publicize the raunchy extracurricular activities of some athletes. It wasn't good for baseball and morals of star-struck youngsters, they argued. The papers didn't object. Words like "gonorrhea" and "syphilis" were unprintable in those days.

In today's post-Freudian, post-playboy jungle of situation ethics, much of society doesn't know the difference between right and wrong. Sex, in particular, is widely held to be permissible between consenting adults or within a "meaningful relationship" where the "meaning" is usually defined by the ego-tripping male chauvinist.

Whatever else sex is today, it is certainly big business. Sex sells toothpaste, automobiles, vacation trips, and especially magazines, books, and newspapers. In the old days the public couldn't be blamed for thinking all athletes were virtuous bachelors or ideal husbands and fathers. Today we're misinformed by the illusion that many (if not most) of our sports champions bounce from bed to bed.

Take a slice from the life of an ordinary sportswriter. The New York Jets are due in town to play the local NFL team. The game itself will be well covered by a half-dozen local sportswriters and photographers. But because the Jets have the colorful, swashbuckling Joe Namath, there will be more story opportunities. Namath is always hot copy for a human-interest story.

"Get me five hundred words on Broadway Joe's sex life," the sports editor barks to his junior scribe.

The writer calls the Jets public-relations director and makes an appointment to talk with Namath. The Jet quarterback is the most sought after member of the team for interviews.

Soon after the Jets check into their hotel, the writer arrives—ahead of time, as one always does for stars like Namath.

He walks to a house phone in the lobby and calls the room number given by the PR man. Namath answers that he'll be down in a minute and they can have a drink together.

An eager feminine voice pleads over the writer's shoulder: "Is Joe coming down to see you? Can we see him, too?" He turns to see three star-struck girls, who look as if they are still in high school.

"Nope, sorry. We have business. And he doesn't have much time."

"Then give us his room number. Nobody else will. We'll go and wait in the hall for him to come back up. Please, mister. Please."

The writer smiles and pulls out his slim reporter's notebook. "Would any of you like to be Namath's girl?" he asks.

"Oh, yeah! Yeah!" they chorus.

"What's he got that other guys haven't?"

"I like the way he walks," says one. "And his eyes. Didja ever see how he looks at you on television?"

"His eyes burn right through you," says another.

"Like he's undressing you?"

"Yeah, yeah! That's it."

"Then you'd say he has sex appeal?"

"Yeah, yeah, man, he's got that all right. Now will you give us his room number?"

"Whatja say your name was? And yours?"

The girls innocently give him their names. Then he sees the shaggy-haired Namath stepping from the elevator. With the girls trailing behind, he walks over to greet Namath, and they go into the darkened lounge. The girls are stopped at the door and turned away because they are obviously underage.

The writer gets only a few grunts, yes's, no's, smiles, and shrugs from the Jet quarterback. Then Namath excuses himself to see a friend he has spotted at the bar.

The next morning a quarter million readers get the impression that girls are standing in line to go out with Namath, that he takes a different one to bed every night. The story is picked up by the wire services and read that afternoon by millions from the Philippines to Lebanon. Three months later quotes appear in several magazine articles, and a year later some of what was written comes out in a book. Actually, some of Namath's close friends, who are in the Christian athlete movement, feel that his playboy image is greatly overblown by the media.

Add more articles, television interviews, and press releases, and you can see how sex myths are created around sports stars. This aura rubs off on the public images of other professional athletes, who don't have the charm and swagger and quarterbacking ability of Namath. That many are happy squares with better morals than the average fan goes unnoticed and unbelieved.

A writer doesn't have to look hard to discover that a sizable number of squarish Christian athletes play for the Jets. They worship together before every out-of-town game in a chapel service begun by their former linebacker Paul Crane, an All-American from Alabama.

Crane was a *Playboy* All-American at Alabama. "I had nothing to say about this," the butter-tongued

33

Southerner recalls. "I knew only a few days before my picture was published in *Playboy*."

Playboy, along with *Time* and other magazines, selects an All-American football team at the end of each season. Like the other publications, *Playboy*'s selections are not based on morality but on gridiron performance. *Playboy* has chosen other Christian athletes whose life philosophies are poles apart from Hugh Hefner's.

Crane's only known "vice" is crossword puzzles. Though tolerant of the views of others (including one of the quarterbacks he snapped the ball to when he was a center at Alabama—Joe Namath), he has established firm guidelines for himself. "At Alabama," he recalls, "Coach Bryant taught me to see everything in terms of black or white—right or wrong."

Paul Crane's "square" Alabama roommate was Steve Sloan, the Crimson Tide quarterback who followed Namath and broke three of Broadway Joe's records.* Sloan never made it big in the pros (his career with the Atlanta Falcons was marred by injuries). But he has done well in coaching. He was at Vanderbilt, but will be coaching Texas Tech in 1975.

In his autobiography, *Calling Life's Signals,* Steve Sloan calls "good friend" Namath a "truly great natural athlete." He also thinks Namath "has been misrepresented" in the press. "It's been implied that he doesn't care about anybody but himself. Joe does care. He's got two bad knees, but plenty of guts.

". . . Just because Joe and I have different ideas about some things doesn't give me the right to cut him down with my tongue," Sloan says. "It's one thing to state your beliefs, and quite another to judge and condemn someone who doesn't agree with you. Sometimes it isn't what you say but how you say it and who you say it about."[1]

Sloan's beliefs about sex are stated plainly in his book.

---

*Most yards passing in a game—226 against Namath's 205; most passes completed in a season—97 against Namath's 76; most yards gained passing in a season—1453 against Namath's 1192.

"I don't think it [sex] should be a hush-hush thing as if it never happens . . . I'm a normal male with a natural sex drive who enjoys fulfillment with my wife Brenda [the high-school sweetheart he married while with the Atlanta Falcons] in marriage relations. I'm interested in sex. I'd be dishonest to say otherwise.

"I believe sex is a gift of God intended to be used within a proper relationship for proper purposes. It is the most sacred and intimate sharing which a man and woman can experience together."[2]

By proper relationship Coach Sloan means marriage, by proper purpose "the procreation of children and/or the sharing of love with the person who is dearest to you. In this sharing your mate must be treated as a person."[3]

Sloan is unbending on the so-called new morality which suggests that in certain situations it may be best to have sex before marriage. "This makes every person his own guide. None of us is smart enough to know always what is right and wrong. Think of God who created the universe, the seasons, the tides, the human body and other marvelous things. It's absurd for anyone to think he is smarter than God. The Bible [with its prohibition against premarital sex] has survived the tests of time and persecution. It still applies to us today."[4]

Tom Landry strongly concurs with Sloan and says, "The Biblical concept that sex belongs within marriage must be maintained for survival."

Big, beefy, All-Pro Bill Glass who carried 255 smashing pounds as a defensive end for the Cleveland Browns until opting for a full-time evangelistic ministry stands with Landry and Sloan. In *Get in the Game,* his first of three books on Christianity and sports, Glass wrote:

Many people have failed to see that sex is a gift from God, and not a god in itself. When we worship a false god, it always turns into a devil that destroys us and others. It's like the man who goes out in the front yard and digs up a little square of sod. He takes that square of sod into the front living room and shakes it until something falls on the beautiful white carpet. What is it? Dirt! In the front yard it's fine and good, and everybody likes it; but in the front living room on the carpet, it's just plain dirt. There are some things that are wonderful and beautiful and good in their place. In the context of marriage, sex is a gift of God. But out of place and before marriage, just plain dirt. Wrongly used sex hurts the possibility for the happiest marriage that you could look forward to.[5]

In his most recent book *Don't Blame the Game* (coauthored with Baptist seminary professor, William M. Pinson, Jr.), Glass fires salvos at the Jets' Joe Namath and Colt quarterback Marty Domres for their published opinions* on casual sex.

To the stated view of Namath and Domres that sex is fun, Glass counters,

People following the fun approach cheat themselves. Sex is strictly fun only if they bump and run. If they care, they risk being hurt. If they don't care, sex often ceases to be fun. Sex apart from love doesn't bring the pleasure sex with love brings. As Harvey Cox says, "Sex is fun, but when it becomes nothing but fun, then pretty soon it is not even fun anymore." . . .

The pleasure approach to life says: Get wealth, enjoy sensual activity. Live for yourself. But if you make your goal serving others, you discover real happiness. You realize happiness is a by-product,

*Namath's *I Can't Wait Until Tomorrow . . . 'Cause I Get Better Looking Every Day* (written with Dick Schapp and published by Random House, 1969) and Domres' *Bump and Run: The Days and Nights of a Rookie Quarterback* (with Robert Smith and published by Bantam Books, Inc., 1971).

not a primary goal. Stop chasing fun and begin serving others out of love and you find genuine joy.[6]

Glass calls the playboy argument that sex outside of marriage is okay in private with consenting adults,

... a hopelessly inadequate approach to sex. It leaves too many questions unanswered. How can reason be depended on to guide people in a relationship as emotional as sex? How can "in private" be maintained when the playboys discuss their sex life openly? "No minors" says the playboy creed. But why? And in fact minors are involved. What teenage boy doesn't know the moral stance of the swinging athletes?[7]

The pro turned preacher further contends that "bump-and-run" sex "reduces people to things," and notes that Namath in his book constantly uses the word "thing" in relation to his women. "The Christian," Glass emphasizes, "cannot consider a person made in God's image as a toy, thing, or object."[8]

Glass and other leaders in the Christian athlete movement counsel thousands of idealistic youths each year. Often the subject is sex. For example, one of Glass's close friends had the following discussion with a small town high-school tackle at a FCA conference.

Boy: "The guys on the team are always bragging about, uh, what they can do with their dates. When they ask me, I, uh, have to stand there looking dumb. Or tell a lie."
Counselor: "You have a girl?"
Boy: "Oh, yes sir. She's a doll."
Counselor: "Have you gone all the way with her?"
Boy: "No, sir. I don't want to do something we both might later regret. But the guys keep bugging me. They seem to think that unless I do, I'm less than a man."

Counselor: "Do you really believe that?"

Boy: "No, sir. But what can I do about the guys?"

Counselor: "I can understand your problem. When I was a rookie in the NFL, I was kidded about my moral convictions. I turned my head away when the language got bad."

Boy: "That wouldn't stop the guys on my team."

Counselor: "You can't make them stop. You'll just have to keep standing for what you believe is right. In the long run they'll respect you as the real man."

Boy: "I guess so."

Counselor: "Project yourself ahead fifteen years from now. Would you want a boy to take advantage of your daughter?"

Boy: "He'd better not try."

Counselor: "Well, I think you know what's right. Let's pray and ask the Lord's help."

The boy and his hero kneel on the grass.

Boy: "Dear Lord, you know how much I want to be liked by the guys. Please help me not to pretend I'm something I'm not. And help me to act like a Christian should when I'm with my girl."

Counselor: "Heavenly Father, Bill here belongs to You. Bless his relationship with his girl. Help him do what is right. Help him, too, in his relationships with the guys on his team. May he stand for what is right, but without a holier than thou attitude. In the name of Christ, Amen."

The two rise and stand for a moment arm in arm.

Boy: "Thank you, sir. I'll always remember this."

Counselor: "And I'll be praying for you when you go home."

The boy returned home to his girl and team. He faced the same temptations to compromise and bend his convictions, but with a new strength and the assurance that he had a friend who understood. He was reassured of this when two weeks after the football season started a note came from the pro counselor asking, "How's your team doing?" And, "How're things with you and your girl? Hope to see you back at FCA camp next year."

"Youth have a terrible time understanding and coping with sex drives," Jerry Stovall says sympathetically. "It's beyond me why adults will not face this sensibly—not only counsel with their children in a Christian atmosphere, but give them love, guidance, and discipline. From what I've seen, coaches are far more concerned about the morals of youth than are parents."[9]

Another veteran counselor of young athletes is old pro Don Shinnick. A college freshman at an FCA conference in Black Rock, North Carolina, tried to put him on the defensive.

"Christianity doesn't sound like fun to me," the freshman said.

"So what do you call fun?" Shinnick retorted.

The boy grinned. "Shacking up with a couple of girls at night. That's fun."

"But what happens afterward? How long does that kind of fun last?"

The boy sobered and settled down to talk about the meaning of life and what is involved in following Christ.

Shinnick met the girl of his future at a Campus Crusade for Christ rally. "She didn't look like a painted doll," he recalls. "She had a sweetness about her that other girls did not have. . . . Both of us had divorced parents, and being next door to Hollywood where some stars changed partners like some football teams change quarterbacks, we wanted an enduring marriage."[10]

Now after seventeen years of marriage, Shinnick has no regrets over "playing by the rules." "The happiness Marsha and I enjoy is more than worth it," he says.

In the same vein, Bill Glass says, "I wouldn't trade my marriage for all the one-night sex stands in the world."[11]

Thus sex for the Christian athletes is reserved for marriage, where they have found it to be a beautiful thing.

CHAPTER FOUR

Right and Wrong

Students from the University of Maine recall that the campus dining hall kept losing tableware until the irate dietician posted a notice on the bulletin board in large, bold letters. The announcement read: "THOU SHALT NOT STEAL," and in parenthesis below, "No matter what Professor Joseph Fletcher says."

The mild-mannered Fletcher is not a household word in sweaty locker rooms. Hearing the name, a lot of players might mistake him for a back who played for the Denver Broncos in the 1960s. Professor Fletcher teaches social ethics at the Episcopal Theological School in Cambridge, Massachusetts. He is best known in the academic world peopled by sociologists, philosophers, and theologians.

But while he may not be a name-drop among many athletes, there are those who view things the same way. Some of Namath's and Domres' published ideas on sex are similar to those in Fletcher's book entitled *Situation Ethics*.

Professor Fletcher argued before an Atlanta seminar on morality sponsored by the Southern Baptist Christian Life Commission that "in the utmost seriousness Christian obligation calls for lies and adultery and fornication and theft and promise breaking and killing— sometimes, depending upon the situation. And that there is, therefore, negatively expressed, no normative principle of conduct which is universally and unexceptionally obliging, regardless of the relativities and circumstances."

Fletcher further told the Atlanta seminar, "I should want to hold that each of the so-called Ten Commandments should be amended with the qualifier word 'ordinarily.' That is to say, usually . . . we ought to tell the truth but not invariably and universally and regardless of the circumstances and the foreseeable consequences."

The professor's "situation ethics" is no new morality, but merely an extention of old ideas, brought to the Western world by Friedrich Hegel. The pace-setting eighteenth-century German philosopher painted a gray area between moral rights and wrongs where he felt decisions can only be made by human conscience.

Hegel's ghost now haunts Western society, especially the youth culture. One of the few pockets of resistance left is organized athletics where the lines between right and wrong are still sharply drawn by Spartan coaches.

The late Vince Lombardi, for example, would have tossed Hegel and Fletcher out on their philosophic ears. The old Packer slave driver might be faulted for his win-at-all-costs program, but he knew that ball games were not won by players wallowing in the mud of moral uncertainties. He used to tell his Packers at the opening of training camp: "Gentlemen, I demand only three things from you: respect and honor for your God and church, faithfulness and loyalty to your family, and a total commitment for a winning team."

Lombardi, a devout Catholic and strict disciplinarian, didn't need to spell out the specifics. The players understood that illicit drugs, drinking, and association with shady characters would not be tolerated.

Paul Brown, the ringmaster for the Cincinnati Bengals, is more specific. He tells his players that if they wish to remain on his team they must avoid the very appearance of vice. They must dress like gentlemen in public, watch their language, and stay out of hotel bars.

Sparky Anderson, whose baseball Reds are co-tenants of Cincinnati's Riverfront Stadium with Brown's Bengals is just as straight-laced.

"I can't forbid my guys to wear beards, for example, but I can ask it," says the neatly groomed Anderson. "If my players don't respect me enough to obey my wishes, I shouldn't be manager.

"I'm not self-righteous or overly religious. But I think kids are hard enough to control without getting encouragement from their sports heroes."

Many college coaches are no less unbending than some of their professional counterparts. Frank Broyles, coach at Arkansas, long-time FCA leader forbids players to indulge in alcoholic beverages during the season. His players' guide specifies, "Any member of this team caught drinking beer or a cocktail will be dismissed from the squad. NO EXCEPTIONS."

Broyles expects his team captains to "know the difference between right and wrong" and to be "shining examples" to players. It is wrong, according to Broyles, "to lie, cheat on an exam, use profanity, develop or keep harmful habits, be intolerant of others' shortcomings, to expect more of your teammates than you do of yourself."

John Wooden, the winningest college basketball coach ever and another FCA stalwart, hasn't used profanity since the sixth or seventh grade when his brother Cat flipped a pitchfork of manure in his face. He lectures his players on drinking, points out the problems it can create for them, and recommends that they not partake during the season. "There was a time in my coaching career when drinking or smoking was automatic dismissal," Wooden notes in his autobiography. "I don't tell my players that now. I tell them that because they are in the public eye and are seen wherever they go. Whatever they do they should feel obligated to set a good example for admiring youngsters."[1]

Wooden is a stickler for conservative appearance. One year when the team assembled for press and picture day, he noticed a pair of extra long sideburns, a goatee, and muttonchops among his players. Looking at his watch, he told the three offenders, "You have twenty minutes to decide whether you're going to play basketball at UCLA this year or not. There are clippers and razors in the training room."

Well within the alloted time the trio was ready to pass inspection.

Another player let his hair grow long and asked Wooden what would happen if he refused to cut it.

"I won't do anything," the coach replied.

"I thought you wouldn't let us wear our hair real long."

"I won't. It's quite all right; you can wear your hair any way you want. I can't determine how long you wear your hair. All I can determine is whether or not you play."[2]

Coaches seldom have disciplinary problems with athletes committed to Christ and the Bible. Smoking is out, because in their view it harms the body, which the Bible calls the "temple of the Holy Spirit." "You were bought with a price" [the sacrifice of Christ], the Apostle Paul also wrote. "So glorify God in your body."[3]

The Christian athletes are unequivocally opposed to drugs for the same reason. Some disdain even those that can be bought with a medical prescription.

Speaking for his sport, the Orioles' third baseman Brooks Robinson says, "With 162 games from April through September, baseball is a day-to-day job, and anyone who thinks he can keep hyping himself up to play better is dreaming. . . . I want no part of the drug scene, and I'm convinced that no one—especially an athlete— can afford to become involved in it. Playing around with drugs will surely destroy whatever talents God has given us."[4]

Most of the Christian athletes do not drink—period. Not even during the off season when they are not supervised by coaches. For example, when Jerry Stovall was an off-season sales representative for the Missouri Portland Cement Company, he often surprised customers and other salesmen by politely declining drinks. "As a

Christian, I don't believe I should indulge," he would say when drinks were suggested.

Stovall recalls taking one contractor to a restaurant where the customer mumbled in response, "Training rules?"

"No," the football player replied, "it's just that I don't believe Christ would want me to drink."

The contractor flushed and said in amazement, "This is the first time in thirty-five years of business that I have seen a salesman turn down a drink. I'll pass up mine today."

Stovall and friends of like conviction don't make a big issue of their teetotaling. As one said, "We don't go around yelling, 'Rah! Rah! for me. I don't drink.'"

Steve Sloan, when a quarterback for the Atlanta Falcons, took the same stance. "I have some good friends who see nothing wrong with taking an occasional drink," he said. "I wouldn't try to judge them or say that I'm a better Christian than they are because I don't drink."[5]

Sloan, however, does feel something should be said about the destructiveness of America's most deadly drug. He points out that alcoholism now ranks with cancer, mental illness, and heart disease among the four major American health hazards; that one person in seven admitted to a mental hospital is an alcoholic; that a drinking driver is involved in about fifty percent of all automobile fatalities; that excessive drinking causes an annual wage loss of around a half billion dollars.

Johnny Oldham, a basketball coach at Western Kentucky University, believes drinking has become too readily accepted in American society. To illustrate, he presents a parody of a brand of hay called "Old Scarecrow" made from locoweed and advertised as an exciting blend of old straw aged in the cornfield.

"Farmers begin buying 'Old Scarecrow' and feeding it to their herds instead of regular feed. The cows lose their senses and run into automobiles. Over twenty thousand are killed and many more are injured every year. Milk production drops because consumers of 'Old

Scarecrow' lose a hundred million milking days a year.

"The life expectancy of cows that eat 'Old Scarecrow' is reduced an average of more than ten percent. Five million cows fall so seriously ill that they are only a drag on the dairy industry. But the makers and sellers of 'Old Scarecrow' keep making bigger and better profits, and for every cow cured ten more bovines become addicts. And the market is allowed to advertise the destructive feed in every pasture by showing pictures of healthy, contented cows, happily munching away on 'Old Scarecrow.' "

Oldham and Sloan believe Christian athletes and coaches should lead the way in alcohol education.

In regard to language, the Christian athletes do not share the same vocabulary with many colleagues. There would be few, if any, "expletives deleted" in a transcript of their conversation, although their earthiness might shock an old ladies Sundayschool class.

Their guideline for language is the New Testament where, for example, Paul wrote, "Let there be no filthiness ... anger, wrath, malice, slander, and foul talk from your mouth."[6]

Cursing for the Christian athlete is a clear violation of the Third Commandment that forbids the taking of the name of the Deity in vain.[7]

Lying breaks the ninth law of the Decalogue.[8]

Long hair, beards, and other deviations from middle-class life-style are seen as cultural mores. The Christian athletes know that Jesus and His apostles wore their hair long. But when coaches insist (and not all do) they go along with rules on the basis of Biblical teaching that authority should be obeyed. Their guide is the apostle Peter who wrote "Be subject for the Lord's sake to every institution."[9]

But the Christian athletes don't like to emphasize negatives. They don't like to be seen merely as "jocks for Jesus" who don't drink, smoke, curse, or wear their hair long.

"Christianity is much more than a call for people to be good," an FCA manual points out. "It is a call for men and women to be disciples of Jesus the Christ. Anything less than this is a total departure from everything taught and demanded by Jesus Himself."

For the Christian athlete, this discipleship governs all his human relationships and responsibilities.

CHAPTER FIVE

Why Christians Are Winners

Stanford University is the type of school that attracts students from the upper grade levels of their high-school classes. Even football players—who are signed by most schools for brawn instead of brains—must meet the scholastic requirements.

The football team may not win many games, but when the diplomas are handed out, corporation recruiters stand in line to acquire their talents.

The 1970 and '71 seasons were exceptions. Stanford won the power-packed Pacific-8 Conference both years and back-to-back Rose Bowl contests over Ohio State and Michigan respectively.

Key players wanted to tell the sports world their winning secrets and requested network television time before the second Rose Bowl game. NBC offered them three minutes, but at the taping cut the time back to forty-five seconds. Then for some unexplained reason the abbreviated player comments were snipped.

The Rose Bowl audience never heard that during the past two seasons many Stanford players had been meeting for weekly prayer meetings before each game—and that over two-thirds of the team had met to pray for the current Rose Bowl contest. As center Dennis Sheehan put it, "Our prayers before a game add to the unity of the team. We give the game to the Lord for His glory and ask that He allow us to tax our physical bodies as well as our mental faculties to perform the best that we can."

The Stanford '70 and '71 teams are not unique. Significant winning records have been attained by other teams studded with key players who are dedicated Christians.

Take the Oklahoma Sooners who won the Big Eight Conference twelve years in a row and posted a college record of forty-seven wins in a row. Bill Krisher played three seasons and was twice an All-American guard while the Sooners were accumulating the record win string in the mid-fifties. He recalls that "almost every player was a committed Christian. They were great because of that," he believes.

Perhaps the greatest football team in UCLA history was dubbed "the eleven from heaven" because so many players were actively involved in the evangelistic ministry of Campus Crusade for Christ. During their undefeated 1954 season, UCLA inflicted record-breaking losses on two conference opponents (72–0 and 61–0 over Stanford and Oregon State respectively) and were crowned national champions by UPI and the Football Writers of America.

Don Shinnick played on that team. He states, "I said then and I say again now that our greatest reason for winning was that seven of the starting eleven and three of the second-string were unquestionably committed to the leadership of Jesus Christ!"[1]

Shinnick was drafted by the Baltimore Colts and played professional ball during the team's glory years. He and his wife Marsha persuaded Bob Vogel, a former Ohio State captain then with the Colts, and his wife Andrea to attend an FCA family conference in North Carolina. The Vogels, who had been only casual church attenders, were turned onto the Bible as a dynamic life guide. Returning to Baltimore, they passed their enthusiasm on to other Colt couples. Result: a weekly Bible study for players and their wives, which soon involved ten to twelve Colt regulars.

Shinnick and Vogel think it not a coincidence that the Colts became a better team after the team Bible study began in 1966. They point out that the team had the second-best record in the NFL in 1967, went to the Super Bowl in 1968, won the Super Bowl in 1971, and played in the American Conference championship game in 1971. Vogel thinks "the spiritual maturity of some of our key players was a significant factor in winning more games. Through our fellowship of Bible study and prayer, we were brought closer together. For instance, when a player would make an error, he would have teammates helping him instead of yelling at him."

Most of the players who formed the nucleus of the Colts' Bible and prayer corps have since retired or been traded. Under new management, the team has suffered through three lackluster seasons and is trying to make a comeback.

Other examples can be cited showing the association of Christian athletes with winning teams. The Green Bay Packers were a dynasty when quarterbacked by Bart Starr. Dallas has rolled under Roger Staubach. The powerful Minnesota Vikings have Fran Tarkenton, Fred Cox, and Jeff Simon. Miami's large contingent of Christian athletes includes Norm Evans, Mike Kolen, Tim Foley, Howard Twilley, Vern Den Herder, Jessie Powell, and others. These four NFL powerhouses are consistent winners.

The record in football strongly suggests that dedicated Christian coaches and players win more games than their non-Christian counterparts.

What about the other major team sports: baseball, basketball, and hockey? The thesis can hardly be supported here because the Christian athlete movement is not as widespread in these sports as in football. However, we can point to certain key players who say that the living out of their Christian faith helps them perform. Take just baseball. Brooks Robinson is the best third baseman in the game. Manny Sanguillen is at least one of the two best catchers, Don Sutton is at the hub of the permament winning Dodger pitching staff, Alvin

Dark led the Oakland A's to a world championship, Don Kessinger has given the Cubs class at shortstop, and injury-plagued Randy Hundley, once with the Cubs and now with the Minnesota Twins, probably tries harder than anybody in the sport.

Nevertheless, Christian athletes do not believe fortune favors them because they are Christians. "We don't think of our faith as a magic talisman," declares Don Shinnick. "But because we follow Christ, we play harder and work together better."

Following Christ to most Americans means little more than church attendance, giving to charity, and conforming to the social code of the community. Sacrifice, discipline, self-control, and do-or-die commitment to group goals spell fanaticism. But this was the language of Christianity before it was watered down by pomp and tradition. Indeed, the New Testament is jeweled with words and symbols of the sports arena: "I press towards the goal to win the prize which is God's call to the life above . . . Train yourself in godliness . . . Fight the good fight of the faith . . . Let us run with perseverance the race that is set before us . . . Do you now know that in a race all the runners compete, but only one receives the prize? So run that you may obtain it. Every athlete exercises self-control in all things . . . Present your bodies as a living sacrifice, holy and acceptable to God."[2]

By changing a few words, these and other statements from the New Testament could go into a coach's manual. The athlete who practices basic Christianity should be able to excel as an individual and motivate his teammates to superior performance.

But the measure of the Christian athlete's faith and spiritual commitment will not necessarily determine his standing on the squad. As Don Shinnick tells aspiring young Christian athletes: "God wants you to be your best. If your best is a third stringer and you reach that goal, then you're a first stringer with God."

Shinnick also emphasizes that the dedicated Christian athlete will do his best even when only God is looking.

He recalls an example that set him to thinking about spiritual matters.

"The summer before I enrolled at UCLA, I rough-necked for an oil company with their first-string full-back Bob Davenport. He was different from any athlete I'd ever known. He joked and laughed, but he didn't curse. He was kind and helpful to me even though he knew I was hoping to win the starting fullback position. But what I especially noticed was the way he cut weeds. Bob always did this job well, while I goofed off and messed around when the boss wasn't on the premises. When Bob told me how he had become a Christian, I listened. Later I asked Christ to come into my life and be my Master."

Years afterward, the lesson Shinnick learned in the weed patch helped the Baltimore Colts win the NFL title in 1958 in the legendary "greatest game ever played." The Colts and Giants were tied 17–17 and playing in sudden-death overtime. On third and six, the Giants' aging quarterback Charlie Conerly saw that his receivers were covered and tried to run Baltimore's left side. Colt linebacker Bill Pellington tackled and slowed him near the first-down marker. Taking nothing for granted, Shinnick moved in from the side and stopped the ball carrier's momentum one *foot* from a first down. In thirteen years of professional play it was probably the biggest tackle assist Shinnick ever made. If he had stood back and not helped Pellington, the Giants would probably have had a fresh set of downs and might have won the game.

While with the Colts, Shinnick helped his closest friend on the squad, Raymond Berry, understand how to become a Christian. Berry had been raised in a Texas church, but had never made a first-time, life commitment. After he did his dedication to Christ spilled over into football. Day after day he stayed after practice to run pass patterns until he could almost run them blind-folded, then squeezed a ball of putty to build strength into his hands. Though he wore contact lenses and couldn't see the big *E* on the eye chart, he became the most sensational pass receiver in the NFL.

"It takes discipline," Berry admitted when asked about the long hours of extra effort put in to perfect his craft. "But my body belongs to the Lord and I want to do my best for Him." Now an assistant coach with the Detroit Lions, Berry is still giving the extra which he feels his Christian commitment demands.

Giving the "extra" also makes the difference between a superior and a has-been lineman in football, according to Bill Glass. The former Cleveland All-Pro estimates that 80 percent of the tackles are made by players who are knocked down but have the grit to get up and try again.

Failure to give this "extra" and keep on top of the game often spells the difference between winning and losing. A pitcher loses his concentration and feeds a home-run ball to a power hitter. A quarterback cocks his arm to pass, then flinches as a brawny tackler bulldozes in. A second later it is too late to get rid of the ball, and he goes down for a disastrous ten-yard loss. In a tie game with seconds to go, a tense lineman is drawn off side for a five-yard loss that proves impossible for his team to make up before yielding the ball to the opponent. A too-eager basketball guard crowds his man too close and commits a fifth foul. A talented golfer takes his eye off the ball for a split second.

Control is the name of the game. The Green Bay Packers while coached by the late Vince Lombardi and quarterbacked by Bart Starr were masters at control. Starr seldom called a heart-stopping, dramatic play. Using bread-and-butter plays, the Packers ground out yardage, seldom fumbling, stayed alert for opponent mistakes, and won week after week.

Starr's bag of records includes: leading NFL passer in 1962, 1964, and 1966, most consecutive passes without interception in NFL (4 percent); and highest carrier percentage of completions in NFL (57.7 percent). He was the NFL's Most Valuable Player in 1966 and Most Valuable Player in 1967 and 1968 Super Bowls.

Starr is certain that "mental and emotional preparedness" wins ball games. "All [NFL] teams are pretty equal physically, so the difference comes in the numbers of errors the players make," he told Gail Habluetsel a writer for Campus Crusade for Christ. "Both teams are going to pull off certain big plays, but the one with the fewest errors is going to win."

A longtime spark plug in the Fellowship of Christian Athletes, Starr feels that one who is "spiritually fit and conerned about others" will be a "better performer in sports because he is at peace with himself." An athlete out of condition spiritually, Starr believes, will be out of balance on the playing field with possible problems and emotional upheavals.

Starr's religious experience was like many other Christian athletes. As a child, he attended church fairly regularly, but did not make a really serious commitment until young adulthood. The catalyst for his commitment was a sorely disappointing loss to the Baltimore Colts in 1958. "As others often do in a time of crisis, I realized my own shortcomings and turned to God for help. As I began to trust more and more in Christ, my life changed. I saw that there are more important things in life than football games."

Starr's good friend Bob Vogel had likewise found spiritual help in controlling his emotions. He played in the Pro Bowl five times and admits that he "used to get very, very angry over things I didn't like. I still get upset, but I've prayed about discipline and read some books and have reached the place where most of the time I'm able to control my emotions, I ask myself: Is this the Christian response I should make? This saves me a lot of embarrassment and helps me be a better witness for Christ."[3]

Christian athletes like Vogel and Starr realize that more is at stake in loss of control than the outcome of a ball game. The integrity of their faith hangs before other players.

Bill Glass will never forget an incident in a game with the Dallas Cowboys. Pained by a sprained ankle, Glass was about to push Dallas ball carrier Don Meredith out of bounds when the Cowboys' Jim Boeke plastered him. As Meredith raced on for another eight yards, Glass yelled angrily to Boeke, "Cheap shot!" He was sure the Cowboy tackler had hit him over the side marker. Just as certain that the tackle was legal, Boeke shouted back, "Glass, you're not even a Christian!"

After the Browns flew back to Cleveland, Glass received a letter from Boeke, not apologizing for the tackle but for what he had said in anger. Then he added the opinion that Glass was the best defensive end "I have ever come up against," and ended, "I hope your ankle heals soon."

Humbled and remorseful, Glass replied that his problem had been frustration over an injured ankle and not with Boeke. Then he closed by hoping that Boeke's Cowboy team would win the championship since the Browns were out of contention.

The Christian athletes are sometimes put under intense pressure by other players intent on breaking their control. Jim Tyrer, the veteran tackler for the Kansas City Chiefs, says frankly, "The environment of professional football is not conducive of religion. It's the pressure, the worry that you'll be proven a hypocrite. It takes a pretty strong person to stand up."

Bill Krisher, who used to play for the Pittsburgh Steelers, sympathetically agrees. At the University of Oklahoma, Krisher had gained a reputation for hard-nosed play and no-compromise morality. His nickname was Crusher. When he got to the NFL, he found his reputation had preceded him.

One Sunday he lined up eyeball to eyeball before a defensive guard across the line. "I hear you're a Sunday-school guy, Crusher," the guard growled, adding a string of curses. "I'm going to hit you so ——— hard, you'll lose your religion."

Krisher returned a toothy grin and said nothing. The ball was snapped. The two collided, shoving and grunting like two buffaloes in a fight to the death. The whistle blew and they pulled back to their huddles. On the next play they slammed together again. For the rest of the game they battled, neither giving a millimeter, each bent on wearing the other down. When the game finally ended, the tempter extended a sweaty paw. "Shake, Crusher. Your religion is as tough as your body."

To win consistently a team must be one for all and all for one. This involves submission to authority, self-sacrifice, cooperativeness, and plain unselfishness—all by-products of Christianity.

The coach sets the example by showing genuine personal interest. John Wooden, who keeps a New Testament on his desk, often tells his players that, next to his own flesh and blood, they are closest to him. "They are my children," he says. "I get wrapped up in them, their lives, and their problems."[4]

Prentice Gautt, a black FCA stalwart and assistant football coach at the University of Missouri, believes that a coach should treat each of his players as he would his own son. A coach who can't do that, he says, should change professions.

The coach in turn must see that team leaders have this sense of caring attitude. Frank Broyles tells his captains, "The quickest way to cause your teammates to lose respect for you is to suddenly develop and display the feeling that you think you are now separate and apart from the other players. If you do not get the full significance of the meaning of humility—consider for a moment some words meaning the opposite of humility—such words as conceit, vanity, and arrogance. Which words had you rather be used in referring to you? The answer to this question should be obvious. It is up to you."

As Steve Sloan reminded his players while coaching at Vanderbilt, "It's the team victory that counts." Based on his experiences in playing and coaching, Sloan believes that the great secret of a team's ability to win consistently is team unity and spirit. "I doubt if a team of All-Americans could win as many games as Alabama has with each man playing for himself," he says.

The Christian athlete is motivated by both his human and spiritual coach to put others first. At this point it is sometimes difficult to determine where the coaching manual ends and where Scripture begins. Take this quotation: "Do nothing from selfishness or conceit, but in humility count others better than yourselves. Let each of you look not only to his own interests, but also to the interests of others ... Do all things without grumbling or questioning ..."[5]

It was not easy for a professional athlete to look "to the interests of others," especially when his own unselfishness may result in loss of his job or early retirement. Consider when Bart Starr was hurt and assigned to teach the Packers' back-up quarterback Scott Hunter. Starr himself never made a comeback. Under his tutelage Hunter became the Packers first-string quarterback. After that Starr faded into the background.

It is not a coincidence that Starr and Hunter were both prepped for the pros at Alabama, where football spells team unity, or that both are spark plugs in the Fellowship of Christian Athletes.

Nor is it a coincidence that winning teams have players genuinely committed to being their best, giving extra, maintaining control, and sacrificing self-interests for the good of the group—all of which are integral to Christian living as outlined in the New Testament.

CHAPTER SIX

Winning Isn't Everything

Organized sports—especially football—are under fire for an alleged win-at-all-costs philosophy that dehumanizes players. A few pros have joined in the criticism. For example, George Sauer said after he quit the New York Jets: "As it is played now, football reinforces the social ethic that aggression and competition is a healthy thing—that that's the way to become a success."[1]

Sauer and other critics single out as Exhibit A the late Vince Lombardi. They point out that he used to say, "Winning is not the most important thing. It is the only thing. If you come off the field defeated, you've lost your manhood."

Lombardi's win philosophy built a dynasty and put Green Bay, Wisconsin, on the map. Few coaches could match the determination, desire, and discipline for winning which the old yardmaster whipped into his players.

Critics may be too severe on Lombardi in calling him ruthless. He was a strict Catholic known to have impeccable morals in his private life. He was not the type to push winning by foul means. Friends think he meant "winning at any price" in terms of personal commitment short of breaking the rules.

Bill Glass is one of those who thinks Lombardi has been misunderstood and unjustly criticized. Glass further feels that brutality in pro football has been vastly overrated by debunkers such as Sauer, Dave Meggyesy, Johnny Sample, and company.

Glass concedes that a player who has a need or drive to play dirty can find an opportunity in football. But Glass "knows" hundreds of players who haven't been brutalized by the game. He claims that in twelve years of line play for the Detroit Lions and Cleveland Browns he never met a tackle who "intentionally tried to injure me." Glass, who played a "rough game," says the object of pro football is not to injure but to outplay opponents. Further, Glass thinks football shouldn't be singled out for special criticism because people are hurt in every type of competition. "The injury is not always physical. It can be emotional. People in business, church work, colleges, the arts are hurt that way every day. . . . You usually get over a physical hurt much faster than an emotional one."[2]

As a defensive end, Glass succeeded best when he broke through the opponent's offense and sacked the quarterback. But the preacher pro insists he never purposely hurt a quarterback when rushing. To the contrary, he says this would have caused him great anguish.

He recalls a time when he thought he had seriously hurt the Atlanta Falcons' Randy Johnson. On the play, Glass got around the offensive tackle with a quick fake and move and bore down on Johnson like a steam-powered bull.

Arm cocked to pass, Johnson was looking hard for an open receiver when Glass rammed into the middle of his back. Glass heard Johnson's neck pop and saw his back bend the other way. Without looking to see where the ball went (the Browns recovered the fumble), Glass leaned over his unconscious opponent, worried that his back might be broken. While Johnson was being carried off the field, Glass "felt like giving up the game." But a few minutes later when he saw Johnson walking up and down the sideline, he was reassured.

Baltimore linebacker Mike Curtis, also known as Animal for his ferocious tackling, isn't much for quoting the Bible, although he respects the Christian athletes.

He defends his game as ardently as Glass, calling the Samples and Meggyesys of pro football a "mirror" of the malcontents in American society. Unlike the gentle Glass, Curtis attacks the game debunkers personally (both Sample and Meggyesy wrote negative books) for alleged dirty play. For example, Curtis charges that after Sample intercepted a pass against the Colts, he pushed the ball into Colt receiver Willie Richardson's face while coming off the field.

The Christian athletes don't have a reputation for such tactics. But they are human and have tempers. For example, cornerback Tim Foley of the Dolphins admits he has become involved in fights on "rare occasions. But when I did, I failed God in not following His teachings of love."

There's no denying that "do back to others whatever they have done to you" is the philosophy of some coaches and players today. A few would make it "do unto others before they do unto you."

Norm Evans recalls having it out with an assistant coach of the Houston Oilers who held to the latter. "You gotta be mean, vicious," he told Norm. "You're out there to hurt the opponent. If you don't hurt them, they'll sure hurt you."

Evans disagreed, but he didn't make a point of it. Later during a game with the Buffalo Bills, he knocked a player down. Getting up, he saw the man was still on the ground, so he reached out his hand and helped him to his feet.

A few plays later when the Dolphins had to punt, Evans trotted to the sidelines. Instead of saying, "Way to go, Norm," the coach began screaming that he should have stepped on the man's hand instead of helping him up.

Evans is now the leader of the Christian athletes on the Dolphins squad. Next to Dolphin quarterback Bob Griese, the big Texas tackle with the hamburger grin is, according to Miami newspaperman Adon Taft, the most popular Dolphin in the Miami area.

He grew up on a dairy farm in New Mexico and

sprouted to six feet, four inches and 200 pounds by the time he was fourteen, a credit to "good, wholesome farm life and running around in fertilizer," his mother says. Though he grew up in a Southern Baptist church, Evans says he "didn't really come to know the Lord" until going to a Bob Harrington revival crusade. "Brother Bob showed Bobbie [his wife] and me that we had head knowledge not heart knowledge. We went forward and asked Christ to forgive us and give us a new life. He did."

The Dolphins noticed that Evans had changed. One day he walked into the dressing room after practice and found a big sign taped across his locker announcing "POPE NORM IV." At first he didn't like the sign, but after thinking about it decided not to make a scene. He soon earned respect for both his playing ability and his faith. Today almost half the squad attends the Sunday before-game chapel which he started.

"Pope Norm" has "lots of fun" playing against Christian brothers. He claims he has the "most fun" against Jerry Mays of the Kansas City Chiefs—now, that is. He didn't have so much fun when the Chiefs and Dolphins collided during his first season with Miami.

The Chiefs were ahead 33–0 when coach Don Shula sent Norm downfield to cover a Dolphins' punt. Suddenly Mays roared in like a freight engine in the fog, and Norm was picking himself off the ground. He was going after the Chiefs' ball carrier, when the engine dropped him again. Getting up once more, he made a second try for the carrier. Bam! Mays again. This time Norm stayed on the ground until the whistle blew.

Norm subsequently found Mays to be a "real Christian gentleman, one who always gives one hundred and ten percent." Whenever the Chiefs and Dolphins meet, the two feud from the opening kickoff. There isn't any animosity, for with every collision the loser compliments the winner. "The reason we get along so well," Norm says, "is that we both know the Lord."

Norm always has a special lookout for Christian

brothers he knows through FCA. Once while playing the Buffalo Bills, his target was the middle linebacker. Coming up on the opponent's blind side, Norm demolished him. Only when he looked down he realized that he had felled "Brother" Harry Jacobs. "Lord bless you, Harry," he called. "How you doing, buddy?" Jacobs broke into laughter.

Later in the game Miami had a long pass intercepted. Norm was bearing down on the interceptor, when he spotted a familiar white jersey heading his way. It was Harry Jacobs eager to smash Norm so he could say, "Lord bless you, Norm!"[3]

The camaraderie endures among other Christian athletes also, even when their teams are blood rivals.

Take a game between the Los Angeles Rams and San Francisco 49ers that had been marked by fights on the field and in the stands. With the Rams leading 26–16 and only five minutes to play, everybody in the stadium was psyched up for the finale. On third down with four yards to go, San Francisco's Steve Spurrier was backpedaling behind his protecting linesmen when the Rams' Jack Youngblood broke through the ranks. Spurrier never had a chance to release the ball as he was slammed to the ground by Youngblood.

Youngblood never hesitated. He reached down for "Brother" Spurrier, pulled him up, slapped him friendly-like on the bottom, and sent him to his huddle with a blessing.

Loving your brother doesn't mean the Christian athletes want to win any less, even when they play against each other. "The Lord don't sponsor no losers," grins Don Kessinger. "No athlete that I know of goes onto a field and tries to lose the game."

At Green Bay, pass receiver Carroll Dale and center Bill Curry were close Christian friends. The two and other Christian Packers used the code PTL—standing for "Praise the Lord"—to communicate during a game. When the yardage was going their way, they would call "PTL"—"to keep us from getting the big head," Dale recalls. When the team took a loss because of a mistake,

"PTL" was a reminder that football was just a game and that spiritual things were of greater priority.

Christians on other pro football teams began using the code. At the end of a hard-fought game victors and losers would shake hands and say the initials that spoke of a deeper comradeship than team loyalty. It wasn't easy after a particularly tough loss, but they said it and always felt better afterward.

One of the toughest "PTL" games was the 1965 play-off for the NFL Western Conference title between Baltimore and Green Bay. There were a number of "brothers" on both teams, and the code signal kept flashing back and forth.

Both Baltimore's first-string quarterback, Johnny Unitas, and back-up signal caller, Gary Cuozzo, were out with injuries and had to be replaced with Tom Matte. Matte's play calling in his high-pitched voice sounded like a sound track from a Walt Disney cartoon show. To top off the dismal outlook, Baltimore line-backer Don Shinnick was playing with one arm in a cast.

But for a while it looked as if Providence favored the Colts. Just after the opening kickoff, Starr drilled a pass to Bill Anderson for ten yards. Then the Colts' Lenny Lyles hit Anderson so hard he fumbled. Incredibly, Shinnick picked up the ball with his one good arm and began running for the end zone. Starr almost had him when Jimmy Welch executed a block that took the Green Bay quarterback out of action for the rest of the game. The Colts were ahead 6–0, and Shinnick had the first touchdown of his pro career.

"PTL," Shinnick shouted to Colt receiver Raymond Berry standing on the sidelines.

Green Bay seemed paralyzed without Starr and gave the ball back to the Colts. Matte moved the Baltimore men close enough for a field goal. Now the Colts were in front 10–0 and could almost taste the conference win.

"PTL," Berry called back to Shinnick as the Colts offensive unit trotted off the field.

After the Packers got a touchdown in the third quarter, the score remained 10–7 until late in the fourth when two disputed calls went against the Colts.

On the first the Colts' Billy Ray Smith was flagged for chopping Packer replacement QB Zeke Bratkowski on the helmet with his forearm. The call canceled an eight-yard Packer loss on the play and moved Green Bay up to the Colt 43.

From there the Pack moved to field-goal range with Don Chandler kicking from the 22. Ignoring the screaming protests of Shinnick and other Colt defenders that the ball had gone outside the goal arms, the official held up his hands for three points. A review of game film later showed the kick had missed, but the points for the Packers held.

Tied at 10–10, the game went into sudden death overtime. Thirteen unlucky minutes (for the Colts) later Chandler kicked the winning field goal that put the Packers in the NFL title game.

The players of both teams were exhausted from the physical exertion and the emotional energy consumed. Carroll Dale and Bill Curry were spilling tears of thanks for the so-much-wanted win. Crossing the field, they met Berry and Shinnick. "PTL," Dale said emotionally. "Well, praise the Lord, anyway," Shinnick grunted back in painful acceptance.

Later Curry joined the Colts in a trade. When the two teams next met (at Baltimore), the Currys invited Carroll over for dinner the night before the game. The two former teammates recalled their "PTL" good times in Green Bay and agreed that no matter who won— Dale's Packers or Curry's Colts—they'd meet after the game and "Praise the Lord" together.

The next afternoon's game belonged to the Packers until the Colts came from behind to win 13–10. When the final whistle blew, the happy Curry ran across the field looking for his good friend. But Dale had run ahead with his teammates in escaping to their locker room.

Curry showered, changed to street clothes, and went

home expecting Dale to telephone. He waited . . . and waited. Finally he went to bed only to be roused by a jangle. Picking up the phone, he heard a subdued choking voice whisper, "PTL." It had been tough, but from nine hundred miles away Dale had kept his promise.

The Christian athletes must have a winning attitude or they could never stay in competition. For this Bill Glass makes no excuses. He thinks that the immortal words of Grantland Rice, so often quoted to console losers, can become a crutch. The syndicated sports columnist wrote,

> When that great scorer comes to write against
>   your name,
> It doesn't matter whether you've won or lost,
> But how you've played the game.

Glass concedes that there's something to taking a loss gracefully, but for himself the former Cleveland All-Pro would rather not take a loss at all. "Good losers usually lose," he says. "It doesn't hurt them enough, so they don't give that last ounce of effort that makes the difference."[4]

Hard-luck baseball catcher Randy Hundley, who was the pizazz of the Chicago Cubs before injuries precipitated a trade, wants to win as badly as Glass. Hundley played under Leo Durocher. Hundley doesn't necessarily agree with Leo that nice guys finish last, but he does think a player "has to be aggressive and think offensively." Thinking positively of yourself and your club means you are more likely to do a good job, Hundley says. Until being crippled by knee injuries, Hundley helped keep the Cubs in pennant competition. Even Durocher felt that nobody worked harder to win than the catcher from Martinsville, Virginia. After Hundley caught Maury Wills and Lou Brock stealing three times each, a sportswriter called him "as good as Sherlock Holmes."

Gary Player, who terms himself a "salesman for God" has a winning attitude in golf. When Player was only twenty, he thoughtfully laid out six major goals for himself: achieving the lowest stroke average for a year on the U.S. professional golf tour; becoming the top money winner on this circuit for a year; and winning the American Masters, the United States PGA Championship, the British Open, and the United States Open Championship.

Within nine years he had attained each goal except for winning the United States Open. His chance to do that came in 1965 at the Bellerive Country Club in St. Louis. If he won, he would be only the third golfer in history to take all four major golf titles and win what was known on the circuit as the "Grand Slam."

He flew into town a week early for practice rounds on the course—the longest on which a U.S. Open Championship had ever been played. All week long he read Reverend Norman Vincent Peale's *The Power of Positive Thinking* and meditated upon Peale's advice to "visualize winning." When he walked past the leaderboard on which all previous U.S. Open winners were listed, he visualized something that no one else saw—the name of Gary Player posted just above Ken Venturi, the previous year's winner. Then he added a prayer for strength and courage to do his best.

When he teed off at the 16th hole he was ahead of Kel Nagle by three strokes. Then came a setback as he took a double bogey while Nagle birdied the 17th to tie the score.

After parring the 17th, Player opened with a tremendous drive on the 18th that put his ball just fifteen feet from the hole. He needed only to par to tie Nagle; a birdie would provide the single stroke needed to win. Cautiously sighting the putt, the South African tapped the ball. While watchers held their breaths, the ball rolled along a line directly toward the cup . . . and stopped one and one-half inches short. He had missed winning by only that much and now had to face an eighteen-hole playoff with Nagle the next day.

Still visualizing his name at the top of the leaderboard, Player went on to win the playoff and attain the coveted "Grand Slam" title. Then he fulfilled a promise made previously and donated his entire $25,000 winnings to charity.

Playing to win doesn't mean that the Christian athletes think they should pray to come out on top. Don Sutton drawls, "A just and righteous God wouldn't want me to pray just for victory. That wouldn't be right on my part." The Dodger pitcher, whom some fans used to mistake for the bat boy, adds, "But I still want to do the best I can. When I came to the Dodgers training camp I was told I had no chance to make the team that spring. I told myself I was going to make it, and I did."

With the kind of desire and dedication that's required to become a major-league contender, it's understandable that losing comes hard.

Ex-Yankee Bobby Richardson, one of the forerunners of the modern Christian athlete movement, will never forget an American Legion game when he was fourteen. His Sumter, South Carolina, team was up against a Legion team from Richmond, Virginia, for a sectional championship. In the eighth inning with the score 3–3 and a man on first, a Richmond batter plunked a ground ball to short. Bobby took the relay throw at second and fired over to first for what he thought would be a sure double play. The Sumter fans yelled in delight, then stilled when the umpire ruled that Bobby's foot had not touched the bag. The runner, safe at second, went on to score what later proved to be the deciding run.

After the game Bobby sobbed out his disappointment to his father. "Believe me, Dad, I stepped on the bag. I really did."

"I believe you, son," his father agreed sadly. "But the official didn't see it that way."

The next day the Sumter newspaper recounted the game and called little Bobby the "goat" of the game. With the pain of losing revived, he turned again to his father for consolation.

This time the elder Richardson was less sympathetic. "Son, you're going to have to learn that when two teams take to the field, one has to lose. You can't win them all."

In the years following Bobby won his share and more. Called "the glue that keeps the Yankees together," he was named outstanding player of the 1960 World Series.

He often described his Christian faith to young audiences numbering in the thousands. "God put me in baseball to play for His glory," he frequently said. "I don't play for the fame of men.

Leaders among Christian athletes today sound the same note. FCA president John Erickson advises young athletes not to "confuse worldly greatness with true greatness. Entering the Kingdom of Heaven is far greater than an undefeated season, a conference championship or a bowl bid," the former coach of the Milwaukee (basketball) Bucks says. "You can spend a whole lifetime in your profession while God says, 'Glorify Me where you are.' True greatness is using the talents He's given you and giving more of yourself."

Going several steps further, Gary Warner, editor of the FCA's *Christian Athlete* suggests that young athletes desiring to live out their faith in the athlete world put five "Christ-inspired qualities" in their "game plan."

1 "Respect the contest, yourself, and your opponent;
2 "Adopt a 'winning is third' concept. That is, a commitment first to doing your best, second to team loyalty, and third to the highest total on the scoreboard;
3 "Determine to enjoy competition, doing whatever it takes for you and the team to have fun at what you are doing. . . .
4 "Determine to make each practice and game a learning experience to better understand yourself and others;
5 "Understand that regardless of athletic shop talk about sacrifice, discipline, commitment and all the rest, unless it is wrapped in an

expressed love for the game and all its partici-
pants, it [the game plan] is meaningless jock
talk."[5]

The small son of Carl Erskine, an old Brooklyn
Dodgers stalwart, put it more succinctly when he was
called on to say a table grace. He ended the prayer, "In
Jesus' name we play."

CHAPTER SEVEN

Everybody's Beautiful

On a soft dewy morning two young athletes, black and white, kneel in the grass behind a gym. The young black is from a big-city ghetto where militants control the turf. The white is from a Southern town where the races still do not mix. Until coming to the FCA conference, he had never sat in a worship service with a black brother. Today he and his black friend will pray, eat, study the Bible, and play together along with several hundred other young athletes of both races. Everybody's beautiful among the brothers.

FCA—the principal catalyst behind the Christian athlete movement—has been multiracial from the start.

To understand why FCA has been interracial requires a short trip back into sports history where everybody wasn't always beautiful.

Until 1947 black baseball players were shunted off to Negro leagues where they played without contracts from payday to payday. The best they could do in the all-white major leagues was sit in the grandstands and even that had been forbidden by some clubs back in the twenties.

Thick-jowled Branch Rickey changed all that. It can be argued that in time blacks would have been accepted into the major leagues anyway. But the indomitable Mr.

Rickey, who later helped start FCA, speeded it up at least a decade.

Baseball enthusiasts will also remember that Rickey originated baseball's foundational farm system, developed the art of scouting, opened baseball's first all-purpose training camp, popularized free admission of children to big-league games thru Knothole Clubs, and hired the first team publicity man. All this from a Bible-toting country Buckeye who went to college with only one pair of pants.

But Wesley Branch Rickey will be most memorialized for breaking the race barrier and signing some of baseball's greatest players who happened to be black.

He was born in 1881 to hard-working Ohio Methodist farm parents. They taught him to believe the teachings of the Bible, to go to church on Sunday, and to be absolutely honest in business dealings. As a teenage book salesman, he returned his first receipts to a widowed purchaser because he felt she couldn't afford the book. Later at Ohio Wesleyan University he cut himself from the baseball team when he discovered his previous play for pay with a local team cancelled his amateur standing and made him ineligible. Even when his former manager denied paying him in hopes that he could stay on the university's team, Rickey insisted that the disqualification must stand.

He was good enough to receive a contract to play minor-league baseball. But before leaving home he promised his mother he would never play on Sunday. His minor-league manager allowed him this "peculiarity," but when he was called up by the Reds, the Cincinnati manager said if he couldn't play on Sunday, he wouldn't play any day of the week.

There was no compromising with Rickey. He left the team, but not baseball. As a public-relations man, administrator, and manager, he left an imprint on the sport that will never be erased. Throughout his long career, he went to the park only three Sundays: once to help a War Bond drive, once to assist the Red Cross, and once to cool a player mutiny.

71

In business dealings his word was his bond, even when it was legal and financially advantageous to break his word. For example, when his Brooklyn Dodgers went into a play-off for the National League pennant, he could have picked up thousands of dollars from radio sponsors because their contract didn't mention the extra games. Rickey insisted that the play-off rights belonged to them anyway.

Rickey's strongest epithet was "Judas Priest," his worst vice, cigar smoking. He could tolerate drinking and cursing from others, but he was implacable about racial discrimination.

Rickey had grown up knowing blacks. The "two smartest kids" in his grammar school had been blacks. But it was while he was baseball coach and director of athletics at Ohio Wesleyan that he became acutely aware of racial discrimination.

He had an outstanding black outfielder named Charles Thomas. When they went to play in South Bend, Indiana, a hotel desk clerk refused Thomas a room. Thomas didn't want to handicap the team and offered to return to Ohio. Rickey was angry and would have none of that. "Put him in my room," he told the manager who, to Rickey's surprise, agreed. Later Rickey was chagrined to learn that a black could stay in many white hotels if he were a servant traveling with a white man.

When they went to the room Thomas sat on the bed, rubbed his hands, and sobbed, "If I could only make them white!" Rickey never forgot that lament.

Years later when Rickey was field manager of the St. Louis Cardinals, Thomas, who had become a dentist, came to see him. Since blacks were not allowed in the grandstand, Rickey boycotted the game and stayed in his office with his old friend. "One day," he vowed to Dr. Thomas, "baseball will change."

Rickey was not one to act in haste. Through the thirties and into the forties he saw that baseball's establishment was almost totally united against integrated play.

72

The Sporting News, baseball's "bible," editorialized that blacks were better off in their own leagues.

Finally, in 1942, he began to lay careful plans. At this time he was president and general manager of the Brooklyn Dodgers. If blacks and whites could fight side by side in a war, he reasoned, certainly the American public would let them play baseball together.

"The war will soon be ending," he told Dodger owners. "We'll need some new, young players." When they agreed that he could start scouts looking for fresh talent, in high schools and colleges, Rickey noted that he might sign "a Negro player or two if we find some good enough. Color has nothing to do with batting power and throwing ability," he added. When they agreed to this, he matter-of-factly pointed out that "a lot of baseball people would be opposed to integration. Will you keep this a secret until I am ready to make an announcement?" They pledged to do so.

When Rickey told his wife his intentions to integrate the national sport, she pleaded, "You're too old."

"No," he replied. "A man never gets too old to obey his conscience."

Rickey's worst critics never intimated that he lacked brains. Having won over the Dodger owners, he looked for a black athlete who would be the right man both on and off the field. The man he selected was Jackie Robinson, who had starred in college football and basketball at UCLA, played baseball in the Negro leagues, and had been an outstanding army officer.

A trusted scout brought Robinson to Rickey's office where the old man said frankly, "We can only win by proving that you're a great ballplayer and a fine gentleman. You'll also need an awful lot of courage."

Rickey then pushed his face close to Robinson's. "Have you got the guts to play the game no matter what happens?" he demanded.

Robinson thought he did.

"All right," Rickey said. "What if . . ." And then he proceded to dramatize what he anticipated Robinson would encounter. First he was a racist pitcher rifling a bean ball that would send the first black player sprawling in the dirt. Then he was a charging base runner, yelling, "Get out of my way, you black s.o.b!" Then a base stealer spiking Robinson in the leg and taunting, "How'd you like that, nigger boy." Then a hotel clerk whining, "Niggers aren't permitted to sleep here." Then a restaurant manager saying that blacks had to eat in the kitchen. And on and on, until in a final pose as an infuriated white player, Rickey swung at Robinson's face with his huge fist.

Without flinching, Robinson merely responded, "I've got another cheek. Is that what you mean?"

"You've got it!" Rickey exclaimed. "You can't fight back—no matter what. You'll have to make it on your ability to play ball—nothing else."

But Rickey wasn't finished. He pulled from his desk a copy of Papini's classic *Life of Christ*. "Read what the Son of God said about nonresistance."

Robinson read some verses quoted from the Sermon on the Mount:

> "Ye have heard that it hath been said, an eye for an eye, and a tooth for a tooth: But I say unto you, That ye resist not evil: But whosoever shall smite thee on thy right cheek, turn to him the other also. And if any man will sue thee at the law, and take away thy coat, let him have thy cloak also. And whosoever shall compell thee to go a mile, go with him twain."[1]

Then a comment from Papini,

> There could be no more definite repudiation of the old Law of retaliation. The greater part of those who call themselves Christians not only have never observed this new Commandment, but have never been willing to pretend to approve of it . . .

Robinson nodded and handed the book back to Rickey. Then he signed the contract and went off to prove himself with Montreal, then a Dodger farm club.

Meanwhile, Rickey was signing youngsters in their teens as replacements for aging Dodgers. Brooklyn fans, loyal to their old heroes, were bitter. They called Rickey "Mahatma." "Deacon," and "Hard-shelled Methodist." The brood of young players were "Mother Rickey's Chickens." One group hanged him in effigy. But all this was nothing compared to the shellacking Rickey received over the signing of Jackie Robinson. The Montreal manager, while having to accept Robinson, asked Rickey if he thought "a nigger was a human being." Montreal games in several Southern cities were sabotaged or cancelled by die-hard segregationists. But Rickey was tenacious and on April 10, 1947, released perhaps the most important press notice in baseball history:

> The Brooklyn Dodgers today purchased the contract of Jackie Roosevelt Robinson from the Montreal Royals. He will report immediately.
>
> Signed,
> Branch Rickey

Significantly, that same year a young assistant coach from Eastern Oklahoma A & M came up with the idea for the Fellowship of Christian Athletes. Don McClanen gave a lay talk in a Presbyterian church on "Making Your Vocation Christian." "It caused me to stop and think about how in the coaching business I could make the most effective Christian witness," he recalls.

During the next seven years McClanen could only "dream" about the idea to friends until it caught fire among a small group of influential clergymen and nationally known sports personalities. The latter included George Kell, Dan Towler, Roe Johnston, Alvin Dark, Carl Erskine, and Branch Rickey. It was Rickey, a genius for recognizing good ideas, who started the ball rolling. "We've got to have an office and a staff," he challenged. When someone mentioned money, Rickey didn't hedge an inch. He got together a group of Pittsburgh businessmen, and they pledged $25,000 for the first year's operation. McClanen was elected the first executive director.

Branch Rickey and the other FCA founders insisted from the beginning that the organization must be interracial, interdenominational, and church-oriented. FCA camps and conferences must not be segregated. Anglos, blacks, Latins, and all other racial and ethnic groups were to be welcomed in the family on an equal basis.

The sports personalities and ministers who found FCA were mostly from Protestant evangelical churches, although the Right Reverend Monsignor Donald M. Cleary, the Roman Catholic chaplain at Cornell University was an early board member. (Catholic participation is much more extensive today.) At the time the constituent evangelical churches were mostly lily-white in membership. These churches—especially in the South —generally felt that blacks and whites should worship separately. Rankled by the just-declared Supreme Court school decision of 1954, some went even further and actively opposed racial mixing on grounds that it was a violation of God's plan for mankind.

Because of FCA's insistence that everybody was beautiful in God's sight, black Christian athletes became involved from the beginning. Dan Towler was one of the starters. When young blacks came to FCA conferences and heard "Deacon" Dan, they knew it was not just another honky church orgamization.

Towler, who had led the NFL in ball carrying in 1952, reaped respect from both blacks and whites. He was a natural leader who

> resolved to throw passes, block, tackle and kick a
> football for the glory of God. And off the field, I
> resolved that my language, my relationships with
> others, the books I read, the company I kept, ev-
> erything would be done for the same reason. As
> the season wore on, I asked the coach one day if

the entire team might pray before each game. Out of 100,000 boys in America who would have given anything to play this game, we had been chosen through the grace of God. Why not kneel before each game and acknowledge that fact?[2]

What coach could say no to that request? Word soon spread around the league that "Deacon" Dan was leading the Rams in prayer. So it was natural that when he was selected to play in the annual Pro Bowl, a teammate from another club would ask, "Dan, how about a prayer before we play?"

"Deacon" Dan Towler was the forerunner of a number of outstanding black Christian athletes who have been active in FCA and the Christian athlete movement.

Prentice Gautt came along in the late 1950s when he was the first black player to integrate University of Oklahoma varsity athletics. (At one time blacks had not been permitted on the streets of Norman—home of the university—after sundown.) Gautt, a powerhouse fullback, ran for 637 yards in 105 carries his sophomore year. Two years later he made several All-American first strings and sparked the Sooners to a 21–6 victory over Syracuse in the Orange Bowl.

Gautt's Christian experience deepened after he signed to play pro football with the St. Louis Cardinals. On a team that had a reputation for bad race relations, he established a close friendship with Jerry Stovall, who was a white defensive back from Louisiana State University. The two started and conducted a Bible study for Cardinal players in training camp. The glue that brought and held them together was their common Christian faith.

When Gautt went to serve on the staff of a summer Fellowship of Christian Athletes camp in North Carolina, he discovered some Southern athletes who felt differently. The first night at the camp, a Mississippi boy began talking loudly about James Meredith's enrollment at "Ole Miss." "I'm at Mississippi State," he said loud enough to make it obvious that he wanted Gautt to hear. "If niggers come there, you can look for bloodshed." The threat stung Gautt. He bit his tongue and said nothing.

Later in the week, on Thursday night, the loudmouth meekly knocked at Gautt's door about 10:30 P.M. "May I talk with you?" he asked softly when Gautt opened the door.

The white boy's attitude had been changed by the prayer and Bible study sessions at the camp. He had been further won over by Prentice Gautt's spirit of love and conciliation. Now he wanted to be a friend and brother with Gautt.

On past midnight the two discussed how Christianity could heal racial hatreds and bring about better relationships between the races. Other young athletes, both black and white, kept arriving and staying to listen. When the discussion finally broke up at 2:00 A.M., the Mississippi boy thanked Prentice and said, "That was the best talk I ever had."

Since becoming a coach, Gautt has kept up his close friendship with Jerry Stovall and other white brothers in FCA. "There are no barriers between us," he says. "Because we're following the same Lord, we understand and trust one another."[8]

Another pair of black-white friends in the Christian athlete movement are Cazzie Russell and Bob Timberlake. They met at the University of Michigan where Timberlake quarterbacked the Wolverine football team, and Russell excelled in basketball. After getting acquainted and discovering that both were Christians, Timberlake confided that he had been "praying about starting an FCA group here." The black athlete from Chicago's South Side grinned and replied, "I've been praying for the same thing."

Together they established the FCA at Michigan, and together as Christian brothers they became an inspiration to students who were searching for ways to bring blacks and whites together.

Similarly Winston Hill and Paul Crane were a black-white inspiration on the New York Jets. Hill is a black offensive tackler from Gladewater, Texas. Crane played under Bear Bryant at Alabama.

One of the best in his position, Hill says without hesitation that the Alabama alumnus who led the team worship service before each Sunday game "has been a strong influence in my life."[4]

"Christians share a common cause," Hill adds. "It's a group therapy of being together and growing together."

Hundreds of other athletes—white and black, high school, college, and pro—are building stronger relationships through such Christian fellowship. They are discovering that, as brothers and sisters in Jesus Christ, "everybody's beautiful."

As Alan Ameche, a stirring hero from the Baltimore Colts' winning yesteryear, put it, "Christianity with us is one big happy family with Jesus as the Head of the house."

CHAPTER EIGHT

Helping Is . . .

Pat Hodgson was an offensive end for the University of Georgia when he first became aware of the adulation kids hold for athletes.

On his way home after a snowfall, he drove between a covey of small boys playing in the snow. Predictably, the small fry bombed his car with snowballs. Pat gave them a nasty look, then forgot the incident until receiving a phone call about three weeks later.

"Pat, you don't know me," a voice squeaked, "but my name is David Quinn. I've been trying to call you, but you were never at home. Do you remember those boys throwing snowballs at your car? Well, we didn't know it was you. Honest, we didn't and we're really sorry."

"That's okay," Pat laughed. "Forget it."

"Gee, that's sure nice of you to feel that way. Er, uh, would it be too much of a favor to give me your autograph? I could come over, well, uh, right now, if you're not going anywhere."

Remembering this plea, Hodgson says, "I would have paid him to come for my autograph. More than that, his words, 'we didn't know it was you,' really stuck with me."

From Georgia, Pat went to the Washington Redskins where he discovered that professional players were even more popular with kids. He noticed that everywhere the team went the small fry swarmed around them for autographs. He also became aware that a few veteran players were ignoring the kids. "Years ago when those guys weren't big stars," an onlooker told him, "they had time to spare for little boys. Now they think their time is too valuable."

The Christian athletes, both the highly publicized stars and the ordinary players whose names seldom appear in the newspapers, take time for young admirers. As Pat Hodgson, who never made it big in pro ball, puts it, "I remember how I felt about a certain high-school football star. I would carry his books, run errands for him, do anything, for I worshiped him." Jim Bakken, kicker for the St. Louis Cardinals, recalls how he treasured the visit of Alan Ameche to his Sunday-school class. "I wasn't much over eight, but I'll never forget Alan speaking to the class. If he had been president of U.S. Steel or some other prominent person, I probably wouldn't have remembered his name. But he was my hero."

The Christian athletes like to include Bible references with their autographs. One of pitcher Jim Kaat's favorites is John 3:16, a Bible verse he learned as a boy, which he says "tells how to start the Christian life":

For God so loved the world, that He gave His only begotten Son, that whosoever believeth in Him should not perish, but have eternal life.

Young autograph seekers unfamiliar with the Bible sometimes misunderstood the Scripture references. When Don Shinnick was with the Baltimore Colts he appendaged John 3:16 to his name on a boy's paper one morning after a workout. Shortly after three o'clock that afternoon the same boy was back. Accosting Shinnick, he pointed to a clock and said, a bit indignantly, "You promised I could see John Unitas at three sixteen. Where is he?"

Paul Crane likes Romans 1:16, which he abbreviates Rm. 1:16:

For I am not ashamed of the gospel of Christ: for it is the power of God unto salvation to every one that believeth . . .

When Crane was at Alabama, one young fan wrote him a thank-you note for his autograph and addressed it to Room 116, Athletic Dormitory, University of Alabama.

Dave Wickersham, who pitched for the then Kansas City Athletics and later the Detroit Tigers, appends Colossians 3:17:

And whatsoever you do in word or deed, do all in the name of the Lord Jesus, giving thanks to God and the Father by him.

Wickersham was acutely conscious of his example while playing baseball. One day he was viewing a game film that showed him arguing with an umpire. Suddenly he realized that fans looking on from a distance might have thought he was cursing the official. After that Wick made a determined effort to avoid a verbal hassle on the field.

But the Christian athletes do more than write Bible verses and try to avoid altercations that young admirers might misunderstand. They try to fulfill their responsibilities to young admirers in other ways. Some examples:

Item: The FCA at Kent State University in Kent, Ohio, with head coach Tom Phillips as adviser, sold their blood to a blood bank and with the proceeds purchased Christmas gifts for orphaned and retarded youngsters at a children's home. But the Kent State group didn't really have a big campus influence until after the 1970 National Guard confrontation against students protesting the U.S. invasion of Cambodia. With four young people dead from the shooting and more violence expected, student radicals tried to close down the university. In response, the FCA athletes organized a "We Care—Kent Stay United Campaign." Five thousand students and university employees wore T-shirts lettered with the slogan and over ten thousand signed petitions asking that the school not be closed. After the crisis was over the university's vice-president credited the Christian athletes with keeping the school open and peaceful.

Item: Every spring a contingent of stars pay their own expenses to Chattanooga, Tennessee, to play charity golf and be dads for a day at Bethel Bible School, a local facility which takes in kids scarred from parental misfortune and neglect. "This is important for me," soccer star Kyle Rote, Jr., says. "We must never be too busy to help kids." Young Rote, whose father was an All-American tailback at Southern Methodist and an All-Pro running back and flanker with the New York Giants, was the leading scorer and Rookie of the Year for 1973 in the American Soccer League. Now a divinity student at Southern Methodist University, he tells young people, "The only way to really live is to be like Christ."

Item: A contingent of Miami Dolphins pedaled from Miami to Disney World for a fund-raising project to provide scholarships for needy young athletes to attend Fellowship of Christian Athletes' conferences. Among the biking Dolphins were Mike ("Captain Crunch") Kolen, Vern Den Herder, Bob Kuchenberg, and Tim Foley. Kolen, a rangy All-American linebacker from Auburn (where he was honored as Defensive Player of the Decade) was co-winner of FCA's Christian Athlete of the Year award in 1970.

Item: Ray May, bachelor linebacker for the Denver Broncos, takes in teen-age boys as foster children. He has had up to three at one time, spending his spare time with them, taking them on trips, and assuming as much as possible the role of a real father.

Item: Down in Vidalia, Georgia, where the days are soft and warm, strong man Paul Anderson and his wife

Glenda have operated a nonprofit youth home since 1961 for teens who have nowhere else to go. To start the home, the Andersons used funds from Paul's personal appearances, shows, and exhibitions to purchase an old mansion and fifty-six surrounding acres of woodland for $32,000. Their first "children" helped paint and repair the old house, and friends in the area contributed money, furnishings, livestock, a truck, a bus, a Volkswagen, and other necessary items.

Having mostly boys, Anderson has constructed an outdoor gym and equipped it with all shapes and sizes of weights and other types of body-building equipment. One boy who weighed in at 115 pounds was soon playing high-school football at 185.

"Our kids come to us underdeveloped and with a lot of problems," he says. "Some have scars burned on their minds before they were six, usually from parental neglect. We give them love and counsel and spiritual guidance. One became a high-school student-body president. Several are in college right now."

Paul Anderson could doubtless make a fortune in show business. But because of his Christian faith he has little desire to become rich. When not at home with his children, he is off giving demonstrations of his unusual strength for the Youth Home (he recently opened another in Dallas) or speaking for the Fellowship of Christian Athletes.

Many other Christian sports stars give their valuable time to the Fellowship of Christian Athletes and other worthy groups. Roger Staubach, for example, has limited his off-season endorsements to products of only three companies and a few paid speaking engagements. He gives the rest of his time to his family, church, FCA, the Salvation Army, Boy Scouts, March of Dimes, the hemophilia fund-raising drive, and to crusades against drugs. When informed that he could earn at least $65,-000 more a year in annual fees if he did less for religion and charity, he responded that there was more to life than making more money.

Baseball's Brooks Robinson also gives a substantial

part of his time for what he considers worthy causes such as the FCA, churches, hospitals, Little League, FCA, and other endeavors. He has been stimulated by FCA since he heard George Kell, the old Detroit Tiger batting ace who led the American League back in 1949, speak at a Baptist church in Little Rock. "As he talked about baseball, his career, and the importance of Christianity in his life, I realized for the first time what an influence professional athletes can have, particularly on young people."[1]

Christian pros like Brooks Robinson, Manny Sanguillen, Don Kessinger, and Don Sutton in baseball; Roger Staubach, Terry Bradshaw, Steve Spurrier, and Fred Cox in football; and retirees such as Bill Wade, Bob Pettit, and Bobby Richardson—to name only a few—are having an immeasurable influence on youth. These and scores of other athletes who identify strongly with Christianity are idolized by millions of hero-worshiping kids.

The influence of the Christian athletes is especially potent when it comes to helping kids understand the basic premises of Christian faith. This was illustrated beautifully by Kerry Donovan, the seventeen-year-old son of Joe Donovan, athletic director, State University of New York. Father and son were returning from an FCA weekend conference where Harry Jacobs and Stu Barber of the Buffalo Bills and other athletes had spoken. "What did you think about it, Kerry?" the father asked. "Dad, I have finally realized what religion is all about," the boy replied convincingly.

Over ten thousand young athletes spend a week each summer at one of FCA's twenty-eight camp conferences, with thousands more participating in athletic clinics, leadership training seminars, community service activities, Big Brother and Sister projects, mass rallies, and local small-group meetings. But it is the week-long conferences that have the greatest impact. Here the young athletes play, pray, and study the Bible with their heros.

What happens can be seen in a sampling of recorded testimonies given at the close of conferences:

I never really believed in God. Felt he did not touch our lives ... Monday I walked the beach and just talked to God. I looked at the ocean and thanked him. Then I noticed the tar and oil along the shore and realized how we could mess up. I experienced God that afternoon. Felt he was talking to me, just to me. I committed my life to him and know I love Jesus with all my heart and soul.

I feel closer to guys I've known four days than some people I've known my whole life.

There is a joy that is nearly unexplainable in playing on a winning team, and when you play on God's team you've won. I've seen strong men fall to their knees and weep this week because they were overcome by the love of God that sent his Son to die for us.

They had us fill out a form and explain why we were coming ... I couldn't be a hypocrite so I wrote "To learn sports from the pros." ... But this week I learned about Christ, also.

It is hard for me to speak in front of a group but I'm going to have to get used to it. In the Quiet Time I talked to God ... But I talked so much I forgot to listen and finally God told me to shut up and listen. I believe he wants me to be a minister. Please pray for me. See you in heaven.[2]

These young men reach a spiritual high through give-and-take interaction and other associations with the Christian athletes who staff the conferences. But what happens when they go home?

Take a boy who came from a Southern high school of about fifteen hundred students where the coaches had reportedly been setting bad moral examples before their players. Parental pressure had finally forced the superintendent to appoint a new head coach. The coach arranged for one of the student ringleaders in delinquency to attend the FCA conference at Black Mountain, North Carolina.

When the boy returned from the FCA meeting, he asked permission to speak to the student body in assembly. "I went to this Christian athlete conference to see my gods in the athletic world," he said solemnly. "While I was there, I heard my gods talking about their God. Before the week ended, their God had become my God."

Later the boy called a local pastor who had led the crusade for the coaching change. "We've got a big game coming up against our chief rival," he said. "Yes," the pastor replied, knowing that in past years it had been the custom for students to go on a rampage of destructive mischief after the game. "If I get the football teams together the day before the game, will you come and pray with us, Pastor? Maybe when the students from both schools hear that we have prayed together, they will not get into trouble after the game."

The pastor met and prayed with the teams as the boy requested. The boy who had attended the FCA camp also prayed that the game would be played clean and that there would be no injuries.

The next day the two teams played without the usual fouling and penalties that had come to be expected of them. And the evening after the game turned out to be one of the quietest the town had known in years.

FCA camp conferences have been targeted mainly at high-school and college athletes, although there are now other conferences which coaches and pros may attend along with their families. Except for a few local programs, not much has been done to reach hard-core delinquents or to work with prisoners. However, some Christian athletes have been involved individually with encouraging success.

Charlie Harraway was chairman of the man-to-man prison rehabilitation program before moving from the Washington Redskins to Birmingham in the World Football League. Harraway, a convert of Tom Skinner, helped enlist community leaders who build one-to-one friendships with prisoners about to be released, then after release continue the supportive relationship.

Bill Glass, the preaching ex-pro, has been involved with prisoners in a different way. A 1974 prison "crusade" took Glass, former Milwaukee Buck McCoy McLemore, former New York Yankee relief pitcher Steve Hamilton, Dallas television sportscaster Bob Kurz, and about thirty-five other laymen to Kentucky State Prison at Eddyville. They held a sports clinic, gave demonstrations of athletic skills, talked about their Christian faith, and counseled individual prisoners. All team members paid their own expenses, including Glass. Inmates and prison staff agreed that it had been one of the best things that had ever happened to the institution.

Glass and another contingent of Christian athletes conducted a prison crusade at the maximum security institution in Waupun, Wisconsin. Among the converts was the warden who pledged to help prisoners set up weekly Bible studies.

Glass wants to take a team of Christian athletes to every prison in America. He believes that "only through purposeful living in Jesus Christ can the issues of life and society be hit head on." By purposeful living he includes being "concerned for others," which, according to Bill Curry, is the "key to all relationships in life."

The Christian athletes would like to enlist other players and coaches in more crusades for helping. Says Brooks Robinson in his autobiography: "I feel strongly that public sports figures must not only support our own area of interest but also provide a helping hand to the many others less fortunate than we."[8]

CHAPTER NINE

Home Sweet Home

During one of the first lulls in a World Series or Super Bowl contest the television producer is likely to turn a camera on player wives. Then the sportscaster gushes, "That's Mrs. Norm Evans in the blue pants suit and Mrs. Bob Griese in the yellow blouse with the butterflies on it. I wish we had time to identify the rest, folks, but they're all beautiful, just gorgeous."

Every player's wife is the envy and interest of countless women who are eager to know how she locked on to Mr. Muscles with his money, fame, and sex appeal.

Here are a few pages from the scrapbooks of four of these wives.

Bobbie Phillips met a future offensive tackle of the Miami Dolphins at a Methodist church meeting when he was in the eighth grade and she in the seventh. But they didn't fall for each other until pairing off at a square dance a few weeks later. After that they had numerous misunderstandings. Once when on a fishing trip with Bobbie and her father, he called her scrambled eggs "marbles," and she responded by throwing off her apron and stomping back to the boat "hopping mad." But love persisted and during his first year at Texas Christian University, she became Mrs. Norm Evans.

Mavis Knapp first heard about a future defensive end of the Cleveland Browns when she complained to her Sunday-school teacher that her dates hadn't been behaving like Christians.

"Oh, they aren't all like that," the teacher assured the tiny, dark-haired freshman. "There's a boy here who lives like a Christian. He teaches a large Sunday-school class, and he plays football, too."

Intrigued, Mavis asked his name. Then she returned to her room, cut out his picture, and pasted it on her mirror. "I'm going to get a date with him," the little freshman told girls who noticed the picture.

This news reached the football player, and one day at "Noonspiration" where a group of students gathered to sing Christian choruses and hymns, another boy tapped her on the shoulder and said, "Turn around and I'll introduce you to someone you've been wanting to meet."

Mavis blushed a spectrum of colors, but she finally managed to sputter, "Hi," then walked away in embarrassment.

That wasn't the end. The next day she ran into him again at "Noonspiration." This time he invited her to play the piano at a church where he was to preach the following Sunday. "I can't play," she admitted. "But I'd like to hear you anyway."

The big football player smiled. "Okay, then I'll pick you up at your dorm early Sunday morning."

After church that Sunday they went to a cafeteria for dinner. Mavis, a green country girl, had never eaten in one before and thought she was expected to sample every item. When the athlete-preacher paid the bill, he remarked, "You ate more than any girl I ever dated."

When he dropped her off at the dorm, Mavis was sure he would never take her out again. Then she was elected a homecoming representative by a campus club. Bolstering her courage, she called her dream man and asked if he would be her escort. To her delight, he consented enthusiastically.

The next year she became Mrs. Bill Glass.

Connie Butcher, a former college homecoming queen, was a United Airlines stewardess on a Baltimore Orioles chartered flight from Kansas City to Boston when she met her future husband. It seemed that every time she came down the aisle one player asked her for more iced tea. As she walked back to the galley the fourth time, he followed. When they reached the galley, he reminded, "I want you to know I'm the only single guy on the plane. Remember, I'm the only eligible bachelor."

"Thanks," she replied. "I won't forget that."

He went back to his seat and pretended to read magazines until his tea glass was empty again. He went back for a refill, and introduced himself by name.

After several more walks between his seat and the galley, they were almost over Boston. "How about having dinner with me tonight?" he ventured.

She was noncommittal, explaining that the crew wouldn't know until check-in at the terminal whether they would be staying over.

When he persisted, she suggested he call her hotel about an hour after landing. He called. They had dinner. Then he returned to his room and told his roommate that he had found the girl he was going to marry.

About two years later she became Mrs. Brooks Robinson.

If the Chicago Teacher's Union had run a beauty contest in 1971, a third-grade teacher named Jill Marie Paige might have won it. She had a perfect smile and deep dark eyes. And her sights were set for the man who was then general manager of the Chicago Bulls basketball team, one of the most eligible bachelors in town.

She was singing in a Billy Graham crusade choir when the young mod sportsman who had stood the town on end with such zany promotions as wrestling a dancing bear before a game stood on the platform and told how he had become a Christian. Right then she decided she wanted to meet him, but the crowds were so big that night she never got close.

She didn't give up. Six months later she read that he was scheduled to speak at Moody Church on the North Side. "I'm going to meet him," she told her mother and left in her car alone.

Her quarry was sitting in the front row signing autographs for kids when she finally reached him. He stood up in respect to a lady. "Would you please sign a program for my third-grade class?" she asked.

He looked at her and said without a break in his voice, "Sure. Now will you sign mine and put your phone number under your name." He thought he was pursuing her.

Though he had been praying to meet the "right Christian girl," he waited over a week to get in touch by phone. She had made a previous commitment and had to say no. The next time he called she was free. When they were better acquainted, he learned she had won a county beauty contest and was a candidate in the Miss Illinois competition, where she was named runner-up for the state title. Three months after the pageant, Jill Marie became Mrs. Pat Williams.

All very exciting and romantic. But what happens after the honeymoon glow is gone? Do the Christian athletes and their wives live happily ever after? Are their marriages any better than those of other celebrities?

Big-time athletes, nationally known politicians, and entertainment stars do have something in common that plagues marriages. It's the celebrity syndrome that boosts egos, invites liaisons with the opposite sex, and encourages self-pity and jealousy from the noncelebrity spouse. It's so bad in politics that Lady Bird Johnson once observed: "A politician ought to be born a foundling and remain a bachelor." It's a fact, for example, that in the 92nd Congress, five legislators from Michigan alone, with seventeen children among them, were divorced. In the entertainment world marital splits have become so common that the lasting marriage has come to be the exception. Marriages of prominent sports figures may on the average be more enduring, but they are still susceptible to the hazards that befall other unions where one spouse is a celebrity.

Take the case of Fred and Elayne Cox. They met at the University of Pittsburgh where Fred was an outstanding running back and kicker. By the time Fred was drafted by the Minnesota Vikings, they were married and enjoying the success which his talented toe brought them.

Fred thought everything was going well until one evening he said something that irritated Elayne. "I'd appreciate it, if you didn't criticize the little things I do," she responded a bit tartly.

That opened up a long discussion in which Fred discovered that life wasn't all kicks for Elayne. Unknowingly, he had taken her for granted, thinking all her needs were being met by money, home, and children. He also learned that he had been habitually finding fault and questioning some of her motives for doing things.

Fred and Elayne were able to talk openly. Fred came to realize that he had brought home the faultfinding from football where criticism was a big part of preparing for games. There he had sat with the Vikings for hours watching game films and listening to coaches analyze each play to determine what had gone wrong.

When he understood what had been happening, he asked Elyane for forgiveness. This opened up a beautiful new relationship between them and with God. Fred asked Christ to take control of his life and live through him. "I got things turned around and in perspective," Fred now says in retrospect. "I put Christ first in my life, the family next, and football third."

He admits he still isn't the perfect husband and father, but "likes to think" he has "come a long way. God has answered my prayers and is giving control. Yet at times I'm still critical. Thankfully, both Elayne and God forgive me.

"We're both more ready to say, 'I'm sorry, I

shouldn't have said that.' Our pride doesn't get in the way as it used to. We're really growing together with Christ at the center of our home. Things run more smoothly now."[1]

Another professional football couple that has found an exciting new relationship in Christian marriage is Norm and Bobbie Evans. They, too, had to learn some things the hard way.

Even when they were high-school sweethearts back in Donna, Texas, as Norm recalls, "We didn't do much else but fuss. We both had plenty of temper."

But they found they couldn't live without each other, and after marriage they wondered at times how they would continue to live with each other.

Then something happened when Norm went to St. Petersburg, Florida, for his first training camp with the Dolphins. Flipping channels on the television, he suddenly stopped at sight and sound of Reverend Bob Harrington, the "Chaplain of Bourbon Street." The preacher wore a red tie, red sox, sported a red handkerchief in his lapel, and held a red Bible. But what held Norm was the answers he was giving to questions being phoned in by viewers. He was assuring them that God could be known as a person and that He cared for people with problems.

The following evening Norm took Bobbie to hear Harrington preach. That night they were converted. As Norm remembers, "We knew all the Bible stories in our heads. We knew that Jesus Christ was the Son of God and had been crucified. But we had never realized that He had died personally for us on the cross. And we had never trusted Him with our lives."

The Evans continued to have rough spots in their marriage. "I felt like a nonperson at times," Bobbie says. "I'm sure all wives of pros have felt that way. I wanted to shout, 'Look, I'm not just Mrs. Norm Evans; I'm Bobbie Evans.' "

Also, with Norm gone so much of the time—for football trips, practice, speaking engagements—she had become resentful of having to be both mother and father at home. When her little boy asked, "Isn't Daddy ever coming home for dinner again?" she went looking for help.

She sought out Marabel Morgan, a Miami attorney's wife who was teaching a course called "The Total Woman" to women in the area.

The vivacious Mrs. Morgan shared with Bobbie what had happened to her marriage. From "strawberries for breakfast and lovin' all the time," the relationship, she said, had drifted to a boring standstill. Realizing something had to be done, she began taking self-improvement courses and studying psychology and the Bible. Practicing principles for building a good marriage had brought "ecstasy" back into her marriage, she said.

Bobbie attended Marabel Morgan's course. She was advised first to accept herself as a beautiful person created by God, accept Norm for "what he is," admire and love him, adapt to his life-style, show appreciation, be "touchable and kissable when he comes home," wear sexy outfits, and develop a sexy attitude. In sum she heard Mrs. Morgan say that when a husband's need for an attractive and available wife was met, he would be grateful and begin to meet her needs.

This reportedly did so much for Bobbie Evans' marriage that eleven other Dolphin wives asked to take the "Total Woman" course.* It may not have been coincidence that the next season the Dolphins became the first team in the history of professional football to win every game, including play-off games and the Super Bowl.

Bobbie Evans now teaches a "Total Woman" course herself. Responding to his wife's new attitudes and ways, Norm now spends more time at home. Every evening when the family is together, they keep the telephone off the hook from 6:30 to 8:30. This is priority time when they pray and study the Bible together and

---

*Marabel Morgan has put the principles of her "Total Woman" courses into a book by that name (published by Fleming H. Revell Co., Old Tappan, N.J.). Many other professional athletes' wives have read it and taken the course. However, there is a growing minority who disagree with the Morgan concept of Christian marriage.

talk with one another and their children, Ronnie and Deana Jo.

According to Norm, they have found that "the closer a couple grows to God, the closer they grow to each other. . . . It's an exciting thing. The Bible has formulas about marriage which we've applied to our lives, and they've worked beautifully."[2]

The secret, both agree, is to "let the Lord be in control." "If He's in control of my life and Bobbie's life," Norm says, "we can't possibly war with each other. When one of us does start getting hostile, then we stand back and see who's in control."

John Small, a 250-pound defensive tackle with the Detroit Lions, has found that the same principle works in his marriage. "When Lucia and I get into an argument, one of us will end up asking, 'Who's on the throne of your life?' Once I said to Lucia, 'God is, but you are trying to get there.' Well, we have differences, but we've found that when each of us sincerely lets God rule our lives, then our relationship becomes beautiful."

The Smalls became close friends with Greg and Connie Brezina when John and Greg both played for the Atlanta Falcons. They made a foursome in studying the Bible together.

The Brezinas became Christians as recently as 1972. Before that they were competing against each other. When Greg went out drinking with his buddies, Connie tried to get even by spending money on clothes. But when they became Christians, Connie says, they came into a "new oneness" with God.

It is this spiritual oneness, the Christian athletes and their wives say, which keeps their marriages intact while other relationships built on lesser values are disintegrating. To paraphrase a tired but true cliché, they are finding that the couple that prays together stays together, and that as time passes the relationship becomes deeper and more meaningful.

CHAPTER TEN

Faith Is the Victory

The cameras always go to the winners' dressing room after the big game. The losers don't want to talk until they've regained their composure and can appear cool and collected. Then it's chin up and "we'll get 'em next time." A competitive athlete must never give his public the impression that he's a quitter.

Dr. Arnold L. Mendell, chairman of the Department of Psychiatry at the University of California School of Medicine, did psychological studies on pro football players and concluded them to be "better adjusted than the average man." Dr. Mendell also found these athletes to be "hypernormal." This is undoubtedly because football players and other big-time athletes have an intensive desire to compete as individuals as well as support their team. It is this, more than anything else, that keeps the truly great athletes playing even while in great physical pain. Who can but admire a Johnny Unitas with broken ribs fading back to pass, or a Mickey Mantle gamely hobbling to first base?

But beneath such mustered courage lurk fears and uncertainties common to all men. Fear of a crippling, career-ending injury. And off the field, all the worries of marriage, family, and personal life that every man faces.

The Christian athletes are not exempt from the vicissitudes and tragedies of life. It is how they respond that makes them different.

Take the experience of catcher Randy Hundley, whose long dark night began early in the season of 1970—a year when many expected the Chicago Cubs to win a pennant. The Cubs' iron man and holler guy hurled himself into the path of 207-pound Carl Taylor as the Cardinal runner was trying to score a game-winning run. (A few days before Hundley had told a reporter, "You can't play this game and be afraid of being hurt. If you do, you're not effective.") Taylor went down in a cloud of dust and was called out, but Hundley lay unconscious on the ground, the ball still gripped in his hand.

A few minutes later he left the field on his own power, acting as though it was just a routine play. Medical examination, however, showed severe knee cartilage damage and he went to surgery. When he was slow in recuperating, Cub manager Leo "The Lip" Durocher lamented, "My losing him is like Cincinnati losing Bench. Hundley does everything. They don't steal against him."

Hundley's attempted comeback later in the season was disappointing. Then to compound his Joblike hard luck, the knee was injured again in the spring. Cub management sent him back to surgery a second time.

The new operation seemed only to aggravate the terrible pain he had been suffering. Lying on his hospital bed, his knee wracked by spasms of pain, he could only watch television in frustration as his team kept losing. Finally the doctors removed his cast and found that swelling had concealed a hidden blood clot. They took him back to the operating room.

Four days later some small clots broke loose and entered his bloodstream, passing through his heart into his lungs. On the brink of death, he lay on the bed, struggling to breathe, heart pounding against his chest.

Up to this time Hundley had been a Christian believer, but not one to bother the Lord about physical aches and pains. When he saw that his wife was really scared, he began asking for help from a higher Physician. After a while he whispered, "Go on home, honey. The Lord will help me with this pain."

Within two hours the pain was almost gone.

But there were more complications. His temperature climbed to 104. His stomach had to be pumped for several days. His right foot ballooned from nerve damage and turned red. Doctors feared gangrene. Then slowly he began to improve and seven weeks later went home with no hope of returning for the season. But that winter he worked his body back in shape and the next year played in 114 games.

Though his leg has never been perfect since, he's thankful for "what God taught me" during the rough road he traveled. "It made me a stronger Christian," he says, "and, I hope, a better person."

Randy Hundley's courage and faith were observed by teammate Ron Santo. The Cubs' All-Star mercurial third baseman had been tormented by botched plays, batting slumps, injuries, and boos. He became discouraged to a point to where he was willing to say, as Hundley had, "I can't make it by myself."

About this time Hundley and shortstop Don Kessinger invited Santo to have a Bible study. Having been raised a Catholic, Santo had always believed in Jesus Christ intellectually, but he was set back by Hundley's question: "Have you received Jesus Christ as your personal Savior?"

"After four Bible studies," Santo recalls, "I realized this was more than believing. I had to ask Jesus Christ to take over all my life. I had to receive Him into my heart."

As Santo continued studying the Bible, a change in his life became evident. Sportswriters noticed that he frequently referred to "the Lord" in conversation. But the fans didn't really become aware until 1971. In the spring of that year he lost both his parents in an auto crash. Later during the season he jolted the sports world by announcing that he had been a diabetic for more than ten years. Pride had kept him from publicizing his diabetes until this time. "I'm different now," he said. "I have a peace of mind I never had before."

But Santo found that his troubles didn't stop after he became a Christian. The following year he broke his wrist and had to warm the bench for several weeks. "It still wasn't easy," he told an interviewer. "But it was easier than it would have been because I knew the Lord was with me."

In 1973 the Cub management decided that the team's future lay in youth. Santo, who had business interests in Chicago, traveled only from the North Side to the South Side where the White Sox put him on second base. As any baseball player knows, changing positions late in one's career is tough. Knowing the past history of Santo, a lot of Chicago fans figured he would get mad and rebel. To their surprise, he accepted the change with grace. "I'm a pro," he grinned, "and a pro can't go around feeling sorry for himself."

No one has ever accused Santo of lacking competitive spirit. His Chicago fans have been heard to say, "Ole Ronnie would pay to play." Ron himself insists his spiritual encounter has not affected his desire. "I go out to win every day. But I don't ask God for hits or home runs. I ask Him to let me do my best. If that isn't good enough to help the team win, then that's the way it has to be." That isn't the old Ron Santo speaking, the Ron who found it almost unbearable to lose.

The agony of a slump can be mentally excruciating. The positions are so few (all the players in the major sports leagues and associations—baseball, football, basketball, hockey, soccer, bowling, golf, etc. could easily be crowded into one small high-school stadium), the pressure from younger athletes trying to break in is so great, and the economic compulsion to keep up an accustomed standard of living so binding that some veterans never make it back. The Christian athletes are most likely to make a comeback because of the calmness and security experienced in their faith.

Consider the story of Mike Durbin, who qualifies for membership in the elite Professional Bowlers' Association. Mike was in his second year on the PBA circuit when his marriage began falling apart. Scared that he would never make it as a husband, father, or bowler, Mike began listening to a fellow bowler, John Coder, who seemed to be joyful even when he was losing.

At the same time Durbin's wife Debbie became friendly with a Christian neighbor woman who lived in their trailer park. Both Coder and the neighbor seemed to be saying the same thing: the secret of living could be found only in Jesus Christ, not in worldly success. Mike and Debbie committed their lives to Christ and began taking their problems to Him for solution. One immediate result was that their marriage relationship turned bright and beautiful.

But his bowling winnings didn't increase. By April of 1972 they were strapped by debt and had to have a big payoff if he was to continue on the circuit. Just ahead was the most lucrative event of the year, the Firestone Tournament of Champions in Akron, Ohio, with a top prize of $25,000.

The Firestone is one of the toughest tourneys on the PBA tour. Entrants bowl sixteen games a day for four straight days, with leaders progressing toward the finals. In the first games it seemed that Mike Durbin rolled a charmed ball. He moved into first place. Then he slipped into second place going into the semifinal position round. He needed badly to roll a high score in the next game to build up a high total for the championship. What he did bowl was a 147, a point total low enough to send a bush-leaguer into a frenzy. He was so despondent he wanted to cry. Walking back after the last delivery, he impulsively started to kick the ball rack in rage when he caught himself.

Durbin went home and for several hours said nothing to his wife. After he finally did open up, she realized along with him that they needed to pray for God's will to be done, not theirs. If God should allow him to make a comeback and win, then the honor would be for God's glory.

The next day, knowing he would be in God's will—

win or lose—Durbin felt buoyant and free. The idea of getting mad never occurred to him. He bowled one of the best three-game series of his career, piling up enough points to win the big trophy and the $25,000 first prize money.

A few minutes later he was asked on national television how the feat had been accomplished. "Without the Lord's help, I couldn't have done it," he replied.

But what happens when the Christian athlete doesn't win? Janet Lynn knows from a heartbreaking setback that occurred when she was only eighteen.

For four years she had practiced daily for the 1972 Winter Olympics in Sapparo, Japan. Confident and poised she swept onto the ice with the goal of taking home the gold medal. The crowd cheered. Everybody was pulling for her.

She did well in the first round of figures and knew it. The rest looked easy: she could imagine herself receiving the coveted award. Then suddenly in the second round she began skating worse than she could ever remember doing in practice. The harder she tried to regain form, the worse she became. When the two-hour break came she went into near hysterics. Her instructor couldn't calm her and her mother had to be called.

She finally got her emotions together and did better during the third round. Then she skated for the exit— still bitterly disappointed, her dream of winning the gold medal crushed.

"Why me, God?" she asked in tears. "Why?" She couldn't understand how years of grueling practice could lead to such humiliation, and she cried and prayed for hours.

Somehow strength came to keep fighting back, and she went into the free skating and won a bronze medal. But the hurt of not winning the gold was still there.

Time proved to be a healing balm. Later she was able to say, "I don't believe I was meant to win the gold. I feel it was more important that I learn a lesson about life and competition. I believe God was pointing out to me that I needed to skate for Him, not for a medal.

Before the free skating I finally determined that I was just going to skate for the Lord. I didn't worry about falling or missing jumps or anything else."[1]

A more mature Janet Lynn is still skating. But Brian Sternberg, who once held the world record in the pole vault, will never again spring into the air, causing the crowds to gasp in admiring awe. He may never even walk again, yet through faith he has found a fulfilling, happy life.

Brian, twenty-one, and a University of Washington sophomore was attempting a double somersault on a trampoline, when, instead of coming down on his hands, he landed on the nape of his neck. He heard a sharp crack in his neck, and lay screaming, "I'm paralyzed! Don't move me."

Doctors could not repair the damage and he came home from the hospital feeling nothing but pain from the neck down.

In the dark days that followed he painfully sorted out his reflections and beliefs. Other Christians, he knew, had suffered freak accidents, contracted diseases that left them invalids, experienced financial setbacks and family tragedies. If God allowed such tragedies to happen to people who loved Him, then He must have a purpose beyond tragedy. Didn't the Bible say, "All things work together for good, to them that love God, to those who are the called according to his purpose?"[2] *God must have some purpose for my life, something left for me to do,* he decided. Clinging to his faith in an all-wise God, he began taking an experimental drug, DMSO (dimethyl sulfoxide). Slowly, feeling began working downward from the head. But it stopped about the level of his armpits.

In August 1963, a month after the accident, an encouraging letter came from President Kennedy who had heard about the tragedy and Brian's determination to make his life count for something. "It greatly disappointed me that you could not join your teammates on the United States track team this summer," the President wrote, "but it is heartening that you are making progress in your recovery. I want you to know that you have been much in our thoughts during these past weeks, and that we hope for continued improvement in the days ahead."

For the next several months Sternberg thought about trying to answer the letter personally. Then when Kennedy was assassinated, he felt he had to write to the President's widow. Letter by painstaking letter, he tapped out the message on an electric typewriter with the middle finger of his right hand.

"The God I have come to know during the past year does nothing and allows nothing that is not in accord with His wonderful Plan of Salvation," he said. "And concerning our respective situations: I am as sure of a reunion with those we love in the life following, as I am of his ability and willingness to heal this life." Then he enclosed an inscribed New Testament.

Brian Sternberg continues as the FCA representative in the Northwest. Still confined to a wheelchair, he "knows" he "could be restored," but says "everything that has happened to me is part of God's will. I would not trade this experience for anything."

The Christian athlete's faith is also operative in family tragedy. As Roger Staubach knows full well. When he was a boy growing up in Cincinnati, family finances were tight. His father, a shoe company representative, was frequently sick and unable to work. His mother worked as a secretary to supplement the family's slim income. But the Staubachs were a warm and close churchgoing family, and today Roger can see God's purpose in the tough times they experienced.

After graduation from the Naval Academy, where he won the Heisman Trophy, the newly commissioned officer married his hometown sweetheart, Marianne Hoobler. Their honeymoon was brief, for he was shipped to Da Nang, South Vietnam, to fulfill his Navy commitment. Though he escaped unscathed from the vicious war, there were moments when he needed to call on the deepest reserves of his faith. One was when the report came that a close friend and Annapolis football team-mate, Tim Holden, had been killed in a battle.

He came home and made a remarkable adjustment to pro football with the Dallas Cowboys after being out of the game for four years. Then just as he was beginning to be enveloped by the aura of greatness, his father died. The following year his fourth child was stillborn. Coming so close to the loss of his father this was "hard to understand" until, as he recalls, "I began to realize that God has a reason for all things. Only when one really begins to suffer does faith take on real meaning."

Carl Erskine can identify with Roger Staubach. The year he retired from baseball, due to constant arm trouble, his wife Betty gave birth to their fourth child. With three "perfect" children, they were shaken to discover that little Jimmy was mongoloid. The doctors could only tell them that his birth was a genetic accident caused by an extra chromosome that could have come from either of them.

Carl had been a charter member of the Fellowship of Christian Athletes and had often spoken publicly of his faith. Yet the birth of a malformed son was hard for him to accept. It turned out that Betty was the strong one. She kept insisting that God had a purpose in bringing Jimmy into their family. She steadfastly refused to take the advice of their family doctor and have their young son institutionalized.

In time Carl adopted her point of view. He resigned from a good job in New York City and moved the family back to his native Anderson, Indiana, where he felt Jimmy would have a better chance growing up as a retarded child. Because there were then no schools in the Anderson area for the mongoloid boy to attend, Carl and Betty determined to teach him all they could. It was a great victory when Jimmy at the age of eight swam part way across the Y pool.

Experiences with Jimmy moved Carl to become active in promoting education and special training for the retarded, both children and adults. One of his happiest responsibilities was helping award medals at the 1973

Special Olympics at Indiana University. It was no less a thrill than pitching in a World Series to put a ribbon around a retarded boy's neck who had just won a fifty-yard dash and was jumping up and down in delight.

Today Jimmy attends a special education school in Anderson, which his father helped establish. He has won awards in Special Olympics competition of the retarded. Classified as "trainable," he will probably one day hold a job involving limited skills.

Carl does not hold back from talking about Jimmy, for he has pride in his son—pride that was engendered by a belief that God never makes mistakes.

The faith that helps Christian athletes through personal difficulties and family misfortune also sustains in the face of death.

Gary Wilson had played basketball with an aching left knee throughout junior high school, high school, and his first year in college in Chattanooga, Tennessee. Doctors said a chipped kneecap had developed into bursitis.

But when he began playing soccer at Tennessee Temple College, he noticed that whenever he touched the outside of the knee, he felt acute pain. It was diagnosed as a transverse cartilage tear. Hospital X rays showed a tumor, and a biopsy indicated malignancy.

His family flew him to New York City where his leg was amputated by the most prominent cancer specialist in the East. Three days later he was in a wheelchair. In the same week he walked on crutches. The therapy nurse called him a superstar.

He returned home with an artificial leg and reentered classes. He cheered his soccer team. He inspired everyone who knew him with his indomitable faith.

On the Sunday before his scheduled graduation, his church, Highland Park Baptist, held "Gary Wilson Day." Gary, then twenty-one, gave a short speech. In sum he said, "When you believe in a sovereign God, then you know there is a reason for everything that happens. My experience only increases my faith in Him."

He died the following August believing what the

apostle Paul wrote to the suffering first-century Christians in Rome: "Neither death, nor life, . . . nor anything else in all creation, will be able to separate us from the love of God in Christ Jesus our Lord."[3]

In life and in death Christian athletes find that only faith can help them experience total victory.

CHAPTER ELEVEN

When Their Playing Time Is Up

What does a baseball pitcher think about after he's won 21 games and posted a 2.96 earned-run average for season? At thirty-six, Jim Kaat, the Chicago White Sox lefty, is wondering how much longer he can last before he must close his locker-room door for the last time. Ten years ago he wouldn't have had these thoughts, for at twenty-six a professional athlete is usually just touching his prime. At thirty-six—if he's still in the game, and not many are—he knows the years are getting shorter. And he has no illusions of being another George Blanda (the Oakland kicker who recently began his twenty-fifth year of pro football).

Kaat recalls that a pro football player once said of his inevitable retirement: " 'His wife will know, his teammates will know, his coach will know, but the player will be the last to know when he's washed up.' "

"I look at older players," Kaat says, "and think 'poor guy: he's all done and doesn't know it.' Then I wonder if they are thinking that about me."

One consolation to aging veterans like Jim Kaat is that it's easier today for retired pro athletes to move into good second careers. This is because most are better prepared to do other things than their predecessors who stayed awake a lot of nights wondering how they would pay the house mortgage. Today, it's an unusual pro football "graduate" who does not have a college degree tucked in with his bag of records when he leaves his game. Many hold master's or even doctor's degrees for swifter advancement into the world outside the great stadiums. The baseball players are also better educated than the previous generation of their genre, most of whom were signed fresh out of high school. During the past decade it's been more the thing to play college baseball first while earning a degree, or to start working on a degree during the first season break.

Nor do most pro athletes wait until sports retirement to begin a second career. When not studying for higher degrees, they build up career credits in a business job. Some earn enough from endorsements and sales commissions to equal what they receive for playing. A few launch big business operations and become millionaires by the time they are ready to hang up their uniforms.

With all these advantages many players still find it traumatic to retire from work that has given them so many satisfactions. They've heard that no one fades so fast as yesterday's hero. They worry about how life will be as a has-been. And if they haven't saved and invested their earnings wisely, they wonder how their families will adjust to a lower standard of living.

At this time it helps to have faith in an all-wise personal God as the Christian athletes do. Not a God to be used as a crutch or a substitute for career planning, but as a guide and support to make the second stage in life as personally fulfilling as the first. Such faith is expressed by Jim Kaat when he says, "I believe God put me in baseball for a purpose, and when the time comes I feel He will have a reason for me being in another field."

Business, coaching, and full-time religious work seem to rank as the top callings of Christian athletes for second careers. A check on twenty who retired from sports within the last dozen years supports this contention.

One of the group, Bill McColl, is an orthopedic surgeon who now practices in California. McColl, a former

All-American from Stanford University, paid his way through medical school by playing football for the Chicago Bears. McColl also served a two-year stint as a medical missionary in Korea.

Another is the Congressional representative of western New York's 38th Congressional District. Jack Kemp, who quarterbacked the Buffalo Bills before plunging into politics, is included in *Time* magazine's two hundred young (under forty-five) leaders of the future who are expected to have great civic or social impact upon America.

Seven of the twenty are in business:

Bill Wade is vice-president of the Fourth National Bank in Nashville, Tennessee.

Jim Ray Smith, four times an All-Pro guard for the Cleveland Browns, sells real estate in Dallas.

Buddy Dial, the guitar-picking offensive end who played for the Pittsburgh Steelers and later for the Dallas Cowboys, is in a ranching partnership in Texas.

Dave Wickersham is an insurance agent in the town where he once pitched for the Kansas City Athletics.

Don Demeter, who led the Philadelphia Phillies in batting (.307) and home runs (29) in 1962, is a Southwestern sales representative for a religious publisher.

Big Al Worthington, one of the best fireballing relief pitchers ever to roll out of a bullpen, is a businessman in his native Birmingham, Alabama.

Clendon Thomas, who led all major college scorers in 1956 and later played for the Rams and Steelers, is in the construction business in Oklahoma City.

Seven are coaches:

Bobby Richardson, who once thrilled Yankee Stadium crowds with his clutch hitting and aggressive defense of second base, is baseball coach at the University of South Carolina. (His boss is athletic director Paul Dietzel, a longtime leader in the Fellowship of Christian Athletes.)

Jerry Kindall, a onetime Chicago Cubs bonus baby and later second baseman for the Cleveland Indians, is baseball coach at the University of Minnesota where he earned All-American honors in the diamond sport in 1956.

Raymond Berry, the "man of a million moves" who held the NFL record in pass receiving before being edged out by another Christian athlete, Don Maynard, coaches the pass receivers for the Detroit Lions. Berry is being considered as a future NFL head coach.

Another head coaching prospect is Don Shinnick, Berry's old sidekick from the Baltimore Colts. Since retiring from the Colts, the onetime UCLA All-American has worked on the coaching staffs of the Chicago Bears, St. Louis Cardinals, and now the Oakland Raiders.

Jim Shofner, an outstanding football player at Texas Christian University and later a cornerback for the Cleveland Browns, tried selling insurance and didn't like it. He is now backfield coach of the San Francisco 49ers and hopes to be a head coach one day.

Six are ministers or otherwise in full-time religious work:

Bill Glass as a full-time evangelist, speaks to crowds of thousands in large churches and auditoriums. Glass, though he is not ordained, earned his graduate divinity degree while playing pro football.

Bill Krisher, twice an All-American guard at the University of Oklahoma when the Sooners were amassing a record string of victories, is Southwestern U.S. Director for the Fellowship of Christian Athletes.

Bob Timberlake, who before playing for the New York Giants was an All-American at the University of Michigan and Most Valuable Player in the Big Ten, is a Presbyterian pastor in Wisconsin. Like Bill Glass, Timberlake attended seminary between playing seasons.

Tony Romeo, an All-American and captain of the Florida State Seminoles in 1959, who later broke a Boston (now New England) Patriots' record for most offensive yardage in a game, also attended seminary during his professional gridiron days. He is now a full-time Baptist evangelist.

Craig Baynham, a track and football great at Georgia Tech who later ran and caught passes for the Dallas

Cowboys and Chicago Bears, is a staff member of Campus Crusade for Christ on college campuses.

Mike Brumley, the All-Star rookie catcher for the Washington Senators back in 1964, is a Southern Baptist pastor. Before his conversion and call to the ministry, Brumley built a reputation for having a fiery temper. "Sometimes, after I struck out," he says tongue in cheek, "they had to redecorate the box seats in back of home plate."

Probably a smaller percentage of Christian athletes decide on a business career than professional athletes as a whole. This suggests that they are more motivated toward service occupations. And even the Christians who do choose business give up large amounts of their time to religious and charitable causes.

The Christian athletes who become coaches see this vocation as an opportunity to influence young men toward God and high moral living. Both they and the Christian-athletes-turned-businessmen frequently speak as lay ministers in churches. Don Shinnick and Jim Shofner, for example, took special seminary courses not to become professional clergy, but as Shinnick explains, "to broaden my knowledge of the Christian faith."

Shinnick has tried to apply his Christian faith by building personal relationships with players. He feels that players want to be valued for other reasons than what they can do on the field of play.

His first coaching job was with the Chicago Bears. Upon arriving in the Windy City, he began making dinner appointments with the defensive players responsible to him. One veteran didn't show up at the restaurant. When Shinnick met him later and asked why, he said, "I thought you were joking, coach. Nobody at the Bears ever did that for me before." Shinnick left the Bears after Abe Gibron replaced Jim Dooley as head coach. (It is customary for a new head coach to name his own staff of assistants.) Afterward, Dick Butkus, then the Bear's superstar linebacker, commented to a reporter that "Coach Shinnick was one of the nicest coaches I ever had. With him you had the feeling that he really cared for you."

Caring is important with UCLA's John Wooden. The coach Wooden "admired tremendously" in this respect was the late Amos Alonzo Stagg, who turned away from the ministry because of speaking difficulties and coached until he was past a hundred years of age. Wooden recalls that the "grand old man of college football" said, "I've never had a player I didn't love." "I'd like to be that way," Wooden says. "I'd like to say I truly loved every player I've had."

The Christian coaches are also helping protect the integrity of sports, particularly on the college level. The FCA surveyed seventy-five Christian college athletes on their concerns over the condition and future of college athletics in America. They saw six crucial problems and issues facing college sports: commercialism, professionalism, overwhelming financial burdens, lack of respect for athletics, recruiting abuses, and the win-at-all-cost syndrome.[1]

Steve Sloan, for example, is concerned about illegal recruiting tactics used by some schools to lure outstanding high-school players into their fold. While at Vanderbilt he said, "I know it goes on, although I don't think it's done as much down here [in the Southeast Conference] as much as, say, in the Midwest. In some cases I would prefer to think that the coach doesn't know about it, that the alumni are violating the rules without the coach's knowledge and consent. Vanderbilt hasn't had the reputation of being a football power. We're trying to improve our situation, naturally. But the biggest thing we have to offer is a good education. We don't hesitate to tell a prospect that we believe his education is more important than football. We go strictly by the rules in recruiting. I don't even want to talk to a kid that thinks money. And if I know, and can prove someone else is cheating, I'll turn them in."

It may surprise those who see men of the cloth as soft-bodied bookworms, that six of the twenty Christian athlete retirees checked have entered the ministry or related religious work. Actually some of the most colorful and courageous ministers of modern times have been former athletes.

Take Mordecai Ham who brought to the pulpit some of the same spirit that made him the victor of many bouts in the boxing ring. Ham had a propensity for charging full-tilt at what he saw as immorality and spiritual indifference. If local ministers where he was holding a crusade became upset over his directness of speech, then so be it.

For example, Ham jumped in the pulpit "ring" in Charlotte, North Carolina, and began "skinning" everybody in sight. That the newspapers and other Establishment voices criticized him worried him not a whit. He merely hurled more brimstone against "drunkenness" among prominent church people and "fornication" in a local high school.

A headlined story about the fornication charge intrigued a local farm boy named William Franklin Graham, Jr. His chief aspiration was to be a big-league baseball player: his hand still tingled from once meeting Babe Ruth. When a neighbor told him Ham was a fighting preacher, he agreed to go hear the minister.

The young athlete was held spellbound and also frightened by the thunder-voiced ex-boxer. When Ham pointed a big finger in his direction, the boy ducked in reflex action behind the hat of a woman in front. However, he continued to attend and before Ham left town Graham made the decision that may have robbed baseball of a great player.

The boy was sixteen-year-old Billy Graham and he was won to Christian commitment by a former athlete.

Today's athlete-ministers are more polished than the inimitable Mordecai Ham or the theatrical Billy Sunday. But their athletic, he-man background—like that of Ham and Sunday—is respected and listened to.

The minister-athletes occupy some of the most prestigious pulpits in the country. For instance, Donn Moomaw, a member of college football's Hall of Fame, is senior minister at the Belair Presbyterian Church just

114

north of Los Angeles. Moomaw's congregation of over twenty-five hundred includes such notables as Steve Allen and former governor Ronald Reagan.

The number of athlete-ministers is growing. Through FCA activity alone over ninety have entered seminary and full-time Christian work. Many others have discovered a "calling" through Campus Crusade for Christ and other nonecclesiastical outreaches.

As ministers, coaches, businessmen, professional men, and in other vocational capacities, the Christian athletes who formerly excited great stadium crowds are making their lives count for their God and the principles in which they believe.

CHAPTER TWELVE

What the Christian Athletes Believe

The Christian athlete movement, represented largely by the FCA, arose outside the structure of any church or council of churches. There is no Christian athlete church, no more than there is a congregation of Christian airline personnel. It is basically a fellowship of Christian believers, whose vocations and interests are wrapped up in the world of sports. Interestingly, a number of similar Christian fellowships has sprung up within several other vocations. These include the Fellowship of Christian Airline Personnel (composed of pilots, airline hostesses, and ground crew), the Fellowship of Christian Police Officers, the Construction Worker's Christian Fellowship, the Christian Legal Society, the Christian Medical Society, the American Scientific Affiliation, the Christian Businessmen's Committee, the Full Gospel Christian Businessmen's Fellowship, and the Christian Women's Clubs.

The various fellowships are lay oriented and interdenominational, and they emphasize the major Biblical doctrines that give Christianity a spiritual unity while minimizing sectarian differences that have fostered denominationalism. This makes it possible for Baptists, Presbyterians, Methodists, Nazarenes, Lutherans, Episcopalians, Catholics, and laity from many other Christian bodies to be in fellowship together around a core of essential Christian beliefs. As Frank Broyles told a FCA conference in Estes Park, Colorado: "My faith is long on trust and short on theological complexities."

In this closing chapter we will present the beliefs that the Christian athletes (and the other lay fellowship groups mentioned above) generally hold and proclaim.

GOD: THE CREATOR

The Christian athletes do not argue the pros and cons of God's existence. They accept it as ordinary men have done so for millennia. They use simple illustrations that appeal to common sense. A sample from coach Steve Sloan illustrates his argument that there "must be a Master Planner behind the world:"

A quarterback's brain gets signals from 130 million light receptors in his eyes, 100,000 hearing receptors in his ears, and 3,000 taste buds in his mouth. As he drops back, his eyes locate an intended pass receiver, flash the message to his brain along nerve highways at 270 miles per hour. His brain acts on this information and in a split second decides that the end is open enough to receive a pass. Another message flashes to his arm muscles telling them to throw the ball. He throws and another completion may go into the books.[1]

MAN: MADE IN GOD'S IMAGE

The Christian athletes move from this premise to speak out against what they consider to be sexism and racism. "The Christian cannot consider a person made in God's image as a toy, thing, or object," Bill Glass says . A woman "must not be treated as an easily interchangeable accessory for sex play. She should not be regarded—or regard herself—as a 'tension easer,' a 'fine bitch,' 'meat on the rack,' or a 'broad.' "

A business that values profits above people, Glass also insists, treats people as things. So does a teacher who has no personal interest in students, a church that regards members as contributors instead of persons in need. So does prejudice that stereotypes people in groups—"All Mexicans are lazy . . . all Negroes are immoral . . . All whites are racists."[2]

MAN: A SINNER

Men who live, work, play, and eat together in family-like proximity find it impossible to fool one another. "We are not necessarily endowed with any extraordinary moral traits," says Fran Tarkenton.[3] The Christian athletes accept the Biblical teaching that the best of men are imperfect and all are sinners.

JESUS! DIVINE LORD

Historically, Christianity has turned on the doctrine that Jesus was more than a great teacher and idealist, that He is God enfleshed in man, divine Messiah, redeeming Savior, and victorious Lord over death and the grave.

There was no compromising on the divinity of Christ when FCA was formed. Branch Rickey and the other founders did not subscribe to the beliefs of some liberal Protestant theologians that Jesus was less than God. Rickey himself recalled an incident early in his career when his belief in the divinity of Christ had been renewed. It began over lunch with his pastor and a visiting churchman who had commented, "Hardly anybody believes in the divinity of Christ anymore." Rickey was shaken and was unable to pray for several days while he searched the Bible and other historical records to determine if his boyhood teaching could have been wrong. When he finally did conclude that the evidence supported the divine uniqueness of Christ as God incarnate, he rebuked his minister for not speaking up.

The Christian athletes continue to hold that Christ was all that the New Testament claims Him to be. Bowie Kuhn, commissioner of baseball, told a FCA national conference at the University of Delaware in June 1973: "The life, death, and resurrection of our Savior remains one of the best documented facts in history. There is nothing I know more certain than that He lived for us and died for us on Calvary. He is as real in this auditorium as He was on that cross and as He always will be in the hearts of those who receive Him."[4]

JESUS: A MAN'S MAN

The painter's projection of the Man from Nazareth as a pale, anemic, kindly "wax saint" with a haloed ring of light around his head is abhorrent to the Christian athletes. "Nobody like that could have walked through a 'lynching mob' without a hand touching Him or thrown over the tables of the money-changers in the temple without suffering immediate reprisal," Paul Dietzel believes. "I submit that Jesus of Nazareth was a strong, healthy, manly-appearing person whose body was firm muscled by honest toil and rigorous discipline."[5]

THE BIBLE: INSPIRED BY GOD

Golfer Gary Player carries two books with him everywhere he goes. One book is a Bible which he "tries to read a portion of every night." The other is Thomas à Kempis' *Imitation of Christ*.

Other Christian athletes pack their Bibles along with their playbooks when they go on the road. Early in the morning while roommates are sleeping or at night before lights out, they read from the world's most cherished book.

They don't spend a lot of time debating over how God "inspired" the writing of the Bible. They simply believe, as Steve Sloan says, that "God speaks to us through this book."

THE CHRISTIAN LIFE:
A PILGRIMAGE OF FAITH, PRAYER,
AND OBEDIENCE

Faith is trust in an all-powerful Person, Jesus Christ. "If He is Lord," Donn Moomaw asks, "how can we become discouraged or despair?"[6]

Prayer is communicating to this person praise, thanks, petitions, and pleas for forgiveness. "Prayer helps me control my emotions and anger," Bob Vogel has found. "We have a manager who always gives us another chance," says Minnesota Twins' pitcher Jim Perry, who won the American League's Cy Young Award in 1970. Alvin Dark, who led the Oakland Athletics into the 1974 World Series, echoes an "Amen." In the fifties Dark was a well-publicized Christian athlete. Then his fiery temper, charges of racism, and marital problems pushed him out of baseball. After his third dismissal as a manager, Dark dropped out of sight for two and a half years and began to pray and study the Bible as never before. He came back with a calm and restored spirit that astonished the sports world. "I had sinned," he confessed. "Then I learned from the Bible that the Lord understands and forgives."

Obedience for the Christian athletes means putting God ahead of everything, even their cherished vocation. "In the past I was ready to give up everything to follow Christ except football," Don Cockroft, kicker for the Cleveland Browns, notes. "Now I can give up football, though I would like to kick as many years as I can. God will show me His plan. When His time comes for me to leave, I will leave. I'll obey. That's the key word—obedience."

Terry Bradshaw, the NFL's first draft choice in 1970, puts it another way. "When an athlete publicly declares his Christian belief, he may be referred to as an athlete who happens to be a Christian. There's nothing wrong with this association. But I feel it is much more important to be a Christian who happens to be an athlete."

Bradshaw's Christian brothers in the sports world agree. They are Christians first and athletes second.

Notes and Sources

The stories and quotes in this book came from three principal sources:

1. Personal interviews with leaders of the Christian athlete movement, including about fifty professional players and professional and college coaches.
2. Published materials (principally *The Christian Athlete*) from the Fellowship of Christian Athletes.
3. Published biographies, autobiographies, and general-interest inspirational books by Christian athletes (see For Further Reading).

Chapter 1

1. Rom. 8:28, King James Version.
2. James C. Hefley, *God on the Gridiron* (Grand Rapids, Mich.: Zondervan Publishing House, 1973), p. 28.
3. *The New York Times*, May 1, 1966.
4. *The Christian Athlete* (publication of the Fellowship of Christian Athletes), December 1973, p. 11.

Chapter 2

1. Matt. 6:25, Revised Standard Version.
2. Matt. 7:24–27, Revised Standard Version.

3. *The Christian Athlete*, December 1966, p. 4.
4. *Ibid.*, April 1973, p. 11.
5. *Ibid.*, March 1973, pp. 4, 5.
6. See John 3:5 and 2 Cor. 5:17.

Chapter 3

1. Steve Sloan, *Calling Life's Signals* (Grand Rapids, Mich.: Zondervan Publishing House, 1967, 1973), p. 87.
2. *Ibid.*, pp. 95, 96.
3. *Ibid.*, p. 97.
4. *Ibid.*
5. Bill Glass, *Get in the Game* (Waco, Tex.: Word Books, 1965), p. 134.
6. Bill Glass and William M. Pinson, Jr., *Don't Blame the Game* (Waco, Tex.: Word Books, 1972), p. 102.
7. *Ibid.*, p. 112.
8. *Ibid.*, pp. 119, 122.
9. James C. Hefley, *Sports Alive* (Grand Rapids, Mich.: Zondervan Publishing House, 1966), p. 46.
10. Don Shinnick as told to James C. Hefley, *Always a Winner* (Grand Rapids, Mich.: Zondervan Publishing House, 1969), p. 65.
11. Glass and Pinson, *Don't Blame the Game*, p. 131.

Chapter 4

1. John Wooden as told to Jack Tobin, *They Call Me Coach* (Waco, Tex.: Word Books, 1973), p. 11.
2. *Ibid.*, p. 165.
3. 2 Cor. 6:19.
4. Brooks Robinson as told to Jack Tobin, *Third Base Is My Home* (Waco, Tex.: Word Books, 1974), pp. 159, 160.
5. Sloan, *Calling Life's Signals*, p. 91.
6. Eph. 5:4.
7. Exod. 20:7.
8. Exod. 20:16.
9. 1 Pet. 2:13, Revised Standard Version.

Chapter 5

1. Shinnick, *Always a Winner*, p. 42.
2. Phil. 3:12, *New English Bible*; 1 Tim. 4:7, 6:12; Heb. 12:1; 1 Cor. 9:24; Rom. 12:1, Revised Standard Version.
3. Hefley, *God on the Gridiron*, p. 93.
4. Wooden and Tobin, *They Call Me Coach*, p. 63.
5. Phil. 2:3, 4, 14, Revised Standard Version.

Chapter 6

1. George Sauer, "The Souring of George Sauer," *Intellectual Digest*, December 1971, p. 52.
2. Glass and Pinson, *Don't Blame the Game*, p. 25.
3. *The Christian Athlete*, October 1970, p. 15.
4. Bill Glass, *My Greatest Challenge* (Waco, Tex.: Word Books, 1968), p. 64.
5. *The Christian Athlete*, September 1973, p. 31.

Chapter 7

1. Matt. 5:38–41, King James Version.
2. Ted Simonson, ed., *The Goal and the Glory* (Old Tappan, N.J.: Fleming H. Revell Company, 1962), p. 93.
3. Hefley, *Sports Alive*, p. 55.
4. *The Christian Athlete*, October 1971, p. 18.

Chapter 8

1. Robinson and Tobin, *Third Base Is My Home*, p. 157.
2. From FCA files.
3. Robinson and Tobin, *Third Base Is My Home*, p. 145.

Chapter 9

1. *Power*, Sunday-school take-home paper for adults (Wheaton, Ill.: Scripture Press, September 15, 1974), p. 3.

2. Norm Evans, *On God's Squad* (Carol Stream, Ill.: Creation House, 1971), p. 84.

Chapter 10

1. *The Christian Athlete*, March 1973, p. 7.
2. Rom. 8:28, King James Version.
3. Rom. 8:38, Revised Standard Version.

Chapter 11

1. *The Christian Athlete*, February 1974, p. 10.

Chapter 12

1. Sloan, *Calling Life's Signals*, p. 60.
2. Glass and Pinson, *Don't Blame the Game*, pp. 22, 23.
3. *The Christian Athlete*, September 1973, p. 7.
4. Simonson, *The Goal and the Glory*, p. 42.
5. *Ibid.*, p. 83.

For Further Reading

The explosion of the Christian athlete movement has resulted in a spate of inspirational biographies, autobiographies, and general-interest books on their careers and work for God. Readers who wish to become better acquainted with their heroes may choose from the following.

AUTOBIOGRAPHIES

Bradshaw, Terry. *No Easy Game*. Old Tappan, N.J.: Fleming H. Revell Publishing Co., 1972.

Evans, Norm. *On God's Squad*. Carol Stream, Ill.: Creation House, 1971.

Glass, Bill. *My Greatest Challenge*. Waco, Tex.: Word Books, 1968.

Lynn, Janet and Dean, Merrill. *Peace & Love*. Carol Stream, Ill.: Creation House, 1973.

Player, Gary. *World Golfer*. Waco, Tex.: Word Books, 1974.

Richardson, Bobby. *The Bobby Richardson Story*. Old Tappan, N.J.: Spire Books, Fleming H. Revell Publishing Co., 1966.

Robinson, Brooks, and Tobin, Jack. *Third Base Is My Home*. Waco, Tex.: Word Books, 1974.

Shinnick, Don. *Always a Winner*. Grand Rapids, Mich.: Zondervan Publishing House, 1969, 1971.

Sloan, Steve. *Calling Life's Signals*. Grand Rapids, Mich.: Zondervan Publishing House, 1967, 1973.

Spurrier, Steve. *It's Always Too Soon to Quit*. Grand Rapids, Mich.: Zondervan Publishing House, 1968.

Staubach, Roger. *First Down: Lifetime to Go*. Waco, Tex.: Word Books, 1974.

Williams, Pat. *The Gingerbread Man*. Philadelphia: A. J. Holman Co., 1974.

Wooden, John, and Tobin, Jack. *They Call Me Coach*. Waco, Tex.: Word Books, 1972.

BIOGRAPHY

Harman, Dan. *Carroll Dale Scores Again*. Anderson, Ind.: Warner Press, 1969.

GENERAL INTEREST

Glass, Bill, and Pinson, William M., Jr. *Don't Blame the Game*. Waco, Tex.: Word Books, 1972.

Hefley, James C. *Play Ball*. Grand Rapids, Mich.: Zondervan Publishing House, 1964.

———. *God on the Gridiron*. Grand Rapids, Mich.: Zondervan Publishing House, 1973.

Warner, Gary. *Out to Win*. Chicago, Ill.: Moody Press, 1971.

———., ed. *A Special Kind of Man*. Carol Stream, Ill.: Creation House, 1973.

FELLOWSHIP OF CHRISTIAN ATHLETES

The FCA publishes *The Christian Athlete* which is available by subscription from the FCA at 812 Traders National Bank Building, Kansas City, Missouri 64106. Information on membership and the various programs and conferences of FCA may also be obtained by writing to this address.